The Executive's Bathroom Companion

Compiled and Edited
By Thomas Patterson

The Executive's Bathroom Companion

Introduction

The idea for this book first struck me whilst sitting in a place one might consider quite appropriate to the topic. Of course, *the idea* being: to provide worthwhile reading material for those most in need of it, during those moments when they are most in need.

At first, the idea seemed strange. But after the initial wave of discomfort, I was astounded by the nuggets of information that sprung forth from the innermost of my being, dropping into the pool of knowledge and leaving ripples of enlightenment as they drifted slowly to the bottom of my consciousness.

Over a long period of struggle, I compiled a collection of tidbits that I am certain will entertain, enlighten and educate the reader. Whether it is motivation, inspiration, humor, or just idle entertainment you are seeking, you will find it in these pages.

It is my fondest hope that I am able to make the time spent reading this book well worth your while. As my dear father always reminded me, "The only real human waste is a waste of time."

Respectfully,

T. P.

Amazingly wrong predictions - Part one

"Inventions have long since reached their limit,
and I see no hope for further development."
- *Julius Frontinus, Roman Empire engineer*

....

"Rail travel at high speed is not possible because
passengers, unable to breathe, would die of as-
phyxia." - *Dionysius Lardner, British scientist (1793-1859)*

....

"This 'telephone' has too many shortcomings to be
seriously considered as a means of communication. The device is inherently of no value to us."
- *Western Union internal memo (1876)*

....

"The Americans have need of the telephone, but
we do not. We have plenty of messenger boys."
- *Sir William Preece, Welsh chief engineer of the
Post Office (1834-1913)*

(continued)

Amazingly wrong predictions (continued)

"Heavier-than-air flying machines are impossible."
- Lord Kelvin, Scottish physicist (1824-1907)

....

"We must not be misled to our own detriment to assume that the untried machine can displace the proved and tried horse."
- John H Kerr, US general (1878-1955)

....

"The talking picture will not supplant the regular silent motion picture." *- Thomas Edison, US inventor (1847-1931)*

....

"I think there is a world market for maybe five computers."
- Thomas J Watson, founder of IBM (1874-1956)

Workforce reduction

Ed worked for a company that was always looking for ways to cut labor costs. Ed remembered the days when there used to be five people working in his control room. As technology improved, the company reduced the staff in the control room to four operators, then three and two, and now Ed found himself working alone all day in front of an electronic control board.

One morning, Ed was shocked to walk into the control room to not only find his manager waiting, but to see a baboon sitting in his chair. A second chair was installed off to the side and Ed's manager directed him to take a seat.

"We spent two months training this baboon to read instructions on the screen and to push whatever buttons he is instructed to push," Ed's boss informed him. "We think this will save us considerable labor costs."

Ed sat for a few hours watching the baboon perform his tasks flawlessly. The screen flashed various messages and the baboon did exactly what the screen instructed.

(continued on following page)

(Workforce reduction, continued)

Ed became more and more worried as hours passed and the baboon continued operating the control panel perfectly. He started to wonder why the company had even kept him in his position.

Then, the screen in front of Ed, which had been dormant all morning, started flashing: "FEED THE BABOON! FEED THE BABOON!"

Feed me

Results follow enthusiasm

A landscape business had been in the family for two or three generations. The staff was happy, and customers loved to visit the store.

A long-standing tradition in the business was that the owner always wore a big lapel badge, saying **Business Is Great!** The business was indeed generally great, although it went through tough times like any other. What never changed however was the owner's attitude, and the badge saying **Business Is Great!**

The badge almost always started a conversation, which typically involved the owner talking about lots of positive aspects of his business and how lucky he was to have such a great business with great customers and employees. Customers always felt a lot happier after just a couple of minutes listening to the owner's enthusiasm.

But when anyone asked what the secret to the business's success was, they would learn the true secret to his successful business. The owner would answer, "The badge came first. The great business followed."

Consultants, Part one

A shepherd was crossing a road with his flock when a passing Mercedes stopped. A man in a business suit jumped out of the car and asked: "What would you give me if I can tell you how many sheep you have in your flock without even looking at them?"

"I'll give you one of my sheep if you can do it," answered the unbelieving shepherd.

At that, the man took out his smart phone and worked for a minute, then announced proudly, "You have exactly 143 sheep!"

(continued on next page)

The shepherd was astonished and said, "Okay, a deal is a deal, go ahead and choose one of my sheep."

The man in the suit quickly grabbed one, placed it in the trunk and was just about to leave when the shepherd stopped him, "If I guess what your profession is, will you return my sheep?"

"That's a deal, but you don't have a chance of guessing it right," smiled the businessman.

The shepherd said confidently, "It's obvious. You are a consultant. First, you come without being invited; then you tell me something I already knew; and last but not least – you took my dog instead of a sheep."

The wisdom of Peter F. Drucker

Peter Ferdinand Drucker was an Austrian-born American management consultant, educator, and author who helped establish the foundations of the modern business corporation. He is one of the best-known and most widely influential thinkers on the subject of management theory and practice. His writings predicted many of the major developments of the late twentieth century, including privatization and decentralization; the rise of Japan to economic world power; the importance of marketing; and the emergence of the information society with its necessity of lifelong learning. He was also considered to have invented the concept known as management by objectives.

Some of his wisdom...

"Rank does not confer privilege or give power. It imposes responsibility."

"What's measured improves."

"People who don't take risks generally make about two big mistakes a year. People who do take risks generally make about two big mistakes a year."

"Executives owe it to the organization and to their fellow workers not to tolerate nonperforming individuals in important jobs."

"Checking the results of a decision against its expectations shows executives what their strengths are, where they need to improve, and where they lack knowledge or information."

"Management by objectives works if you first think through your objectives. Ninety percent of the time you haven't."

"Innovation opportunities do not come with the tempest but with the rustling of the breeze."

"So much of what we call management consists in making it difficult for people to work."

"There is nothing so useless as doing efficiently that which should not be done at all."

"People in any organization are always attached to the obsolete - the things that should have worked but did not, the things that once were productive and no longer are."

"Management is doing things right; leadership is doing the right things."

Ideas for Better Business

Try this technique to evaluate a new business idea

Step 1: Create two independent points of view to examine the problem or the need

As the saying goes, "Two heads are better than one but three are even better." Appoint two parties beside yourself to evaluate the problem. The two parties can be individuals or teams, but in any case they will offer at least one point of view that is different from yours. This has the benefit of creating consensus. If others are involved in the decision, subsequently they will be much more motivated to implement it. Obviously it is important to choose the most appropriate people for the case.

Step 2: Consider the "failure" scenario

After choosing the best version of the decision, imagine that the important decision has failed. Ask each of the parties to answer these two questions: (a) what do you foresee are the 3 to 5 possible factors which led to failure? (b) what are the consequences and costs of the failure?

Too often, once a course of action is chosen everyone tends to shift into "positive mode" and is blinded as to the risks and roadblocks that lie ahead. This exercise is a good way to smoke those out before proceeding.

It is better to request this in writing rather than in a discussion. Oftentimes, no one is willing to confront the positive expectations of the group. Written comments are more likely to be independently thought out and not be subject to peer influence.

Step 3: Finalize the decision and take action

If an honest assessment of risks and downside are made and still favor taking action, then proceed. However, if Step 2 revealed strong negative outcome possibilities, do not view re-boot as a failure. Failure would be a decision that produced horrendous results six months later. Killing a poor decision before action is taken is being far-sighted.

Quotable quotes

"Why join the navy if you can be a pirate?"
- *Steve Jobs*

"Right now, this is a job. If I advance any higher, this would be my career. And if this were my career, I'd have to throw myself in front of a train."
- *Jim Halpert, The Office*

"There's no reason to be the richest man in the cemetery. You can't do any business from there."
- *Colonel Sanders*

"The only place success comes before work is in the dictionary." - *Vidal Sassoon (also attributed to many other sources)*

"The brain is a wonderful thing. It starts working the moment you get up in the morning and does not stop until you arrive at the office."
- *Robert Frost*

"We don't have a monopoly. We have market share. There's a difference."
- *Steve Ballmer, CEO of Microsoft*

"Catch a man a fish, and you can sell it to him. Teach a man to fish, and you ruin a wonderful business opportunity." - *Karl Marx*

"Don't worry about people stealing your ideas. If your ideas are any good, you'll have to ram them down people's throats." - *Howard Aiken*

◆◆

When it's better to go with the winner...

An American touring Spain stopped at a local restaurant and while having a drink, he noticed a delicious looking platter being served at the next table. He asked the waiter, "What is that you just served?"

The waiter replied, "Ah, you have excellent taste! Those are bull's testicles from the bull fight this morning. They are a great delicacy!"

◆◆

◆◆

The American was a bit taken aback, but thinking about how delicious the plate looked and feeling adventurous he said, "What the hell, bring me an order!"

The waiter replied, "I am so sorry, there is only one serving per day because there is only one bull fight each morning. If you really have your heart set on trying it, come back tomorrow morning and I will make sure we save them just for you."

The next morning, the American returned and placed his order. Within minutes the waiter brought out the one and only serving of the special delicacy of the day. After inspecting the contents of his platter and taking a small bite, he called to the waiter and said, "These are delicious, but they look a little different than the ones I saw you serve yesterday."

The waiter shrugged his shoulders and replied, "Si senor. Sometimes the bull wins."

◆◆

Career aspirations achieved

There was once a young man who, in his youth, professed his desire to become a great writer.

When asked to define "great" he said, "I want to write stuff that everyone will read, stuff that people will react to on a truly emotional level, that will make them scream, and cry out in pain and anger!"

He now writes error messages for a software company.

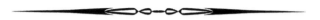

Risk taking

It is not the critic who counts; not the man who points out how the strong man stumbles, or where the doer of deeds could have done them better.

The credit belongs to the man who is actually in the arena, whose face is marred by dust and sweat and blood; who strives valiantly; who errs, who comes short again and again, because there is no effort without error and shortcoming; but who does actually strive to do the deeds; who knows great enthusiasms, the great devotions; who spends himself in a worthy cause; who at the best knows in the end the triumph of high achievement, and who at the worst, if he fails, at least fails while daring greatly, so that his place shall never be with those cold and timid souls who neither know victory nor defeat.

From a speech by Theodore Roosevelt, made in Paris, April of 1910

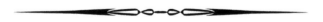

The wisdom of Anne M. Mulcahy

Anne M. Mulcahy is former chairperson and CEO of Xerox Corporation. In addition to the Xerox board, she has been a member of the boards of directors of Catalyst, Citigroup, Fuji Xerox and Target.

Mulcahy joined Xerox as a field sales representative in 1976 and rose through the ranks, later serving as vice president for human resources, chief staff officer, vice president of customer operations and corporate senior vice president before becoming CEO.

The Wall Street Journal named Mulcahy one of Fifty Women to Watch in 2005 and *Forbes* magazine ranked her at the sixth position among the Most Powerful Women in America in 2005. In 2008, she was selected by *U.S. News & World Report* as one of America's Best Leaders.

Some of her wisdom...

"You should be accumulating really great relationships throughout your career."

"When you have that window of opportunity called a crisis, move as quickly as you can, get as much done as you can. There's a momentum for change that's very compelling."

"I have zero tolerance for people who don't come completely prepared. I expect contribution, I expect attendance, and I expect directors to take trips and visit the company's programs."

"Most of my career has been in sales. I spend fifty percent or more of my time with customers and employees, and I can't wait for it to be more than fifty percent."

"We're long past having to defend or explain why women should be on boards, given all the data that shows how companies with female as well as male directors perform better. It's unfortunate when companies with a large percentage of women constituents don't reflect that in their boardrooms."

"You have to live the mission... love what you do."

"Employees who believe that management is concerned about them as a whole person - not just an employee - are more productive, more satisfied, more fulfilled. Satisfied employees mean satisfied customers, which leads to profitability."

Overheard between caddies and golfers

Golfer: If I hit one more shot like that, I'm going to drown myself in the lake.

Caddy: Do you think you can keep your head down that long?

Golfer: I'd move heaven and earth to break one-hundred on this course.

Caddy: Try heaven, you've already moved most of the earth.

Golfer: Do you think I can get there with a 5-iron?

Caddy: Eventually.

Golfer: You've got to be the worst caddy in the world.

Caddy: I don't think so sir. That would be too much of a coincidence.

***

Golfer: Please stop checking your watch all the time. It's too much of a distraction.

Caddy: It's not a watch - it's a GPS.

***

Golfer: How do you like my game?

Caddy: Very good sir, but personally, I prefer golf.

***

Golfer: This is the roughest hole I've ever played on.

Caddy: This isn't the golf course. We left that five strokes ago.

The super high-tech watch

An eccentric looking young man is struggling through the airport with two huge and obviously heavy suit-cases when a stranger walks up to him and asks, "Have you got the time?"

The young man puts down the suit-cases and glances at his wrist. "It's a quarter to six," he says.

"Hey, that's a nice watch!" exclaims the stranger.

The young man's face brightens. "It's amazing! If you think those new smart watches they're talking about are cool, check this out!"

The young man proceeds to show him features that smart phone and smart watch designers could only dream about. The display was not only unbelievably high quality, but could produce a 3-D hologram. And the watch had flawless voice recognition capabilities.

The stranger is struck dumb with admiration and de-sire. "I must have that watch!" he said.

"It's not ready yet, this is just a prototype," said the young inventor. "But look at this," and he proceeds to demonstrate even more amazing features.

26

"I've got to have this watch!" says the stranger, think-ing of the millions he could make if he could have it reverse-engineered and mass produce it. "I'll give you $20,000 for it!"

"Oh, no, I've already spent more than that."

"I'll give you $50,000 for it!"

"But it's just not ready yet!"

"I'll give you $150,000 for it!" And the stranger pulls out a checkbook.

The young man stops to think. He's put about $20,000 into materials and development, and with $130,000 in profit he can finish his schooling and get an engineering degree, unencumbered by student loans.

The stranger finishes writing the check and waves it in front of the young man. "Here it is, a check ready to hand to you right here and now. $150,000. Take it or leave it."

The young man reaches a decision. "It's a deal," he says, and peels off the watch. The stranger grabs the watch and starts to walk happily away.

"Hey, wait a minute!" the young man says as he points to the two huge suitcases he'd been wrestling through the airport, "Don't forget the batteries!"

Know your business buzz words
Part one

Rock star – a talented employee

Thought leadership – expertise in a given area

Do more with less – an edict to produce better results with fewer resources

Make it happen – an inspiring send-off to a minion embarking on an impossible project

Takeaway – important point from a presentation

Pivot – a corporate change in direction

Adult in the room – a person known for level headed decisions and maturity

Big data – gargantuan databases

Care and feeding – interaction with customers that requires minimal effort

Going forward – refers to the future, generally when the past has not gone well

Which way the pickle squirts – asserting authority or power, as in, "I explained to him which way the pickle squirts."

Office terms of yesteryear

Forty years from now, will people remember some of the popular office gadgets being used today? Do you believe the day will come when few people will remember what a "mouse" was? If you doubt that, try your hand at matching the office gadget to the description.

1. Used to make one or more copies of a typed page
2. Was often made of silk and was stored in a disc-shaped tin
3. The long black roller inside of a typewriter
4. Shaped like a pencil with a rubber tip on one end and brush on the other end
5. Small rubber item, thimble-shaped and covered with rubber nubs
6. Dark blue sheet with a light colored stripe on one end and white type

A. Typewriter eraser
B. Platen
C. Ditto Master
D. Carbon paper
E. Paper Sorter
F. Typewriter Ribbon

(Answers on following page)

Answers to Office Terms of Yesteryear

1. D. Carbon paper could make up to three or even four copies, depending on how many you could pile up and jam into the typewriter. Each copy was progressively lighter and lower quality.

2. F. Typewriter ribbons were initially made of silk and for years were stored in a disc-shaped metal tin to keep the ink from drying out.

3. B. A platen was the long roller that also served as a hard backing to the paper.

4. A. Typewriter erasers also had a small string on the rubber end that would be pulled to expose more of the rubber eraser tip as it wore down. The brush was used to whisk away eraser bits.

5. E. Paper sorter. It was common to wear these on two finger tips, usually thumb and forefinger.

6. C. Ditto master was an inky sheet that was covered temporarily with a thin sheet of white paper. You typed onto the white sheet but the impression showed on the blue as white type. The light colored strip on the end was to affix the ditto master to a slot in the ink drum on the ditto machine, the predecessor to today's copiers. Anyone over the age of 40 knows the distinctive odor and blue type of a mimeographed copy.

Innovation

"Always remember that someone, somewhere is making a product that will make your product obsolete." - *Georges Doriot*

"Once an organization loses its spirit of pioneering, and rests on its early work, its progress stops."
- *Thomas J. Watson*

"Originality is something we constantly clamor for, and constantly quarrel with." - *Thomas Carlyle*

"My father worked for the same firm for twelve years. They replaced him with a tiny gadget. It does everything my father does, only it does it much better. The depressing thing is my mother ran out and bought one." - *Woody Allen*

Thoughts about reputation

"The way to gain a good reputation is to endeavor to be what you desire to appear."
- *Socrates*

"Make three correct guesses and you will establish a reputation as an expert."
- *Laurence J. Peter*

"That's what Rocky Balboa is all about: pride, reputation, and not being another bum in the neighborhood."
- *Sylvester Stallone*

"I have the reputation of being easygoing. But inside, I'm like nails. I will kill."
- *Calvin Klein*

"I'm stingy and I'm proud of the reputation."
- *Ingvar Kamprad, Founder and CEO of IKEA*

"A brand for a company is like a reputation for a person. You earn reputation by trying to do hard things well."
- *Jeff Bezos, Amazon.com*

"Our reputation is more important than the last hundred million dollars."
- *Rupert Murdoch*

"Repetition makes reputation, and reputation makes customers." - *Elizabeth Arden*

"You can't build a reputation on what you are *going* to do." - *Henry Ford*

The wisdom of Bill Gates

Born in 1955, in Seattle, Washington, famed entrepreneur Bill Gates began to show an interest in computer programming at age thirteen. Through technological innovation, keen business strategy and aggressive business tactics, he and business partner Paul Allen built the world's largest software business. In the process, Gates became one of the richest men in the world.

Some of his wisdom...

"If I think something's a waste of time or inappropriate I don't wait to point it out. I say it right away. It's real time. So you might hear me say 'That's the dumbest idea I have ever heard' many times during a meeting."

"If I'd had some set idea of a finish line, don't you think I would have crossed it years ago?"

"Success is a lousy teacher. It seduces smart people into thinking they can't lose."

"Just in terms of allocation of time resources, religion is not very efficient. There is a lot more I could be doing on a Sunday morning."

"Before you were born, your parents weren't as boring as they are now. They got that way from paying your bills, cleaning your clothes and listening to you talk about how cool you thought you were. So before you save the rain forest from the parasites of your parent's generation, try delousing the closet in your own room."

"It's fine to celebrate success, but it is more important to heed the lessons of failure."

"Your most unhappy customers are your greatest source of learning."

"I think it's fair to say that personal computers have become the most empowering tool we've ever created. They're tools of communication, they're tools of creativity, and they can be shaped by their user."

"The Internet will help achieve 'friction-free capitalism' by putting buyer and seller in direct contact and providing more information to both about each other."

Marketing techniques

A man sees a gorgeous woman at a conference. He has an arsenal that includes the following marketing techniques to win her over:

He could approach her and say, "I am very rich. Go out with me!" That's direct marketing.

He could ask a colleague to refer him and tell the woman, "He's very rich. You should go out with him." That's advertising.

He could find out her telephone number and then call the next day to say, "I'm very rich. Go out with me." That would be telemarketing.

■ · · ■ · · ■ · · ■ · · ■ · · ■ · · ■ · · ■ · · ■ · · ■ ·

He could send her a link to his website that includes his income and phone number. That's e-marketing.

He might get up and straighten his tie; then walk up to her and pour her a drink and say, "By the way, I'm very rich. Will you go out with me?" That's public relations.

If he's lucky she may walk up to him and say, "I know you from somewhere. Would you like to go out with me?" That's brand recognition.

If he's lacking in marketing skills, he might simply approach her and say, "Hey you, go out with me!" And she slaps his face. That's customer feedback.

■ · · ■ · · ■ · · ■ · · ■ · · ■ · · ■ · · ■ · · ■ · · ■ ·

Thoughts about success

"Success is not final, failure is not fatal: it is the courage to continue that counts."
— *Winston Churchill*

"If at first you don't succeed, try, try again. Then quit. No use being a damn fool about it."
— *W.C. Fields*

"Try not to become a man of success. Rather become a man of value."
— *Albert Einstein*

"So be sure when you step
Step with care and great tact.
And remember that life's
A Great Balancing Act.
And will you succeed?
Yes! You will, indeed!
(98 and ¾ percent guaranteed)
— Dr. Seuss, *Oh, The Places You'll Go!*

"Success is getting what you want,
happiness is wanting what you get."
— *W.P. Kinsella*

"Failure is the condiment that gives success its
flavor." — *Truman Capote*

"If A is a success in life, then A equals x plus y plus
z. Work is x; y is play; and z is keeping your mouth
shut" — *Albert Einstein*

"The worst part of success is trying to find someone who is happy for you."
— *Bette Midler*

"Success is stumbling from failure to failure with
no loss of enthusiasm."
— *Winston Churchill*

Know your business buzz words
Part two

Change management – brand of management applied when a company is in a state of upheaval

Client-facing – work that requires direct interaction with customers

Deliverables – the desired end results of a completed project

Punch a puppy – to perform a necessary task for which you will be detested

Parking lot – holding place for ideas which management intends to address but probably never will

Share of wallet – amount of money extracted from customers

Take ownership – become officially responsible for the outcome of a task or project

Onboarding – training a new employee

Alignment – a pretentious form of "agreement" as in "the customer and I came to alignment."

Fail – slang term for a hideous failure, as in "that was an epic fail."

Gamification – adding content to a presentation or web site that provides a game-like experience

Monetization – often used in reference to online businesses, selling versus giving away information, services or products on a web site

Crowd funding – raising money for a business in small amounts from a large pool of people

Data mining – extracting actual useful information from Big Data

Clueless traveler complaints

Thomas Cook Travel and the Association of British Travel Agents compiled a list of the most off-the-wall complaints made by travelers. Some highlights:

"When do they turn on the Northern Lights?"

"Is there a bridge to Hawaii?"

"It took us nine hours to fly home from Jamaica to England. It took the Americans only three hours to get home. This seems unfair."

Complaint from a visitor to Spain: "There were too many Spanish people there. The receptionist spoke Spanish, the food was Spanish. No one told us that there would be so many foreigners."

"My boyfriend and I booked a twin-bedded room but we were placed in a double-bedded room. We now hold you responsible for the fact that I find myself pregnant. This would not have happened if you had put us in the room that we booked."

"I was bitten by a mosquito. The brochure did not mention mosquitoes."

"They should not allow topless sunbathing on the beach. It was very distracting for my husband who just wanted to relax."

"I'm sure I've stayed in this hotel room in a previous life. I cannot stay here again."

"Our honeymoon was ruined when, on a visit to the zoo, my new bride and I observed an elephant that was in an aroused state. This triggered severe feelings of inadequacy in me, which in turn ruined the honeymoon."

"The beach was too sandy."

"No one told us there would be fish in the sea. The children were startled."

A British guest at a Novotel hotel in Australia said his "soup was too thick and strong." The manager's investigation revealed the guest was eating from the gravy boat.

Courtesy Thomas Cook and the Association of British Travel Agents

Match the business giant
to the accomplishment

1. His first business was a nine-seat root beer stand in Washington D.C. that he parlayed into a hospitality chain of a different sort

2. He was selling a 5-spindle shake machine when he joined two brothers in 1955 to become a restaurant legend

3. This man moved from New York to San Francisco during the Gold Rush, and ended up being known for making garments

4. After being thrown out of college, he inherited his father's ailing business and turned it into a media empire

5. A produce salesman who became so successful in oil refining that he is remembered as being the catalyst for the Sherman Antitrust Act

6. In 1992, this person became the youngest CEO up to that time to lead a Fortune 500 company

A. John D. Rockefeller
B. J. Willard Marriott
C. Ted Turner
D. Michael Dell
E. Ray Kroc
F. Levi Strauss

Answers to business giant quiz

1. B. J. Willard Marriott opened an A&W franchise in 1927, expanded it to several locations by 1932, and opened his first motel in 1957. In 1935 he was diagnosed with cancer of the lymph nodes and given six months to live, but survived another half-century.

2. E. Ray Kroc called on the McDonald brothers drive-in and liked the concept so much that he used the name and business model to launch McDonald's.

3. F. Levi Strauss's family that owned a dry goods store in Kentucky. When the Gold Rush came, they decided to open a California store and sent Levi to open it. He was approached for a loan by a young man who had invented a process for riveting the waist of canvas pants, and partnered to start Levi Strauss & Company.

4. C. Ted Turner inherited his father's failing billboard business in Atlanta and turned it into a worldwide media empire.

5. A. John Rockefeller's company, Standard Oil, gained such an overwhelming market share in oil refining that the government passed the Sherman Antitrust Act which was aimed at breaking up the monopoly that Rockefeller had built.

6. D. Michael Dell was the youngest CEO of a Fortune 500 at the age of 27 in 1992 when Dell Computers reached that lofty status. He still holds the record, but is followed closely by Mark Zuckerberg , who was 28 when facebook hit the Fortune 500.

....

Thoughts about success

"Sometimes it takes a good fall to really know where you stand." — *Hayley Williams*

"All you need in this life is ignorance and confidence; then success is sure." — *Mark Twain*

"The way to get started is to quit talking and begin doing." — *Walt Disney*

"A man is a success if he gets up in the morning and gets to bed at night, and in between he does what he wants to do." — *Bob Dylan*

"It is hard to fail, but it is worse never to have tried to succeed." — *Theodore Roosevelt*

"Success is most often achieved by those who don't know that failure is inevitable."
— Coco Chanel, *Believing in Ourselves: The Wisdom of Women*

....

....

How insurance works

The entrepreneur called his wife with the news that his entire factory had burned down and was a total loss. "While I inspect the damage, can you call the insurance company?" he asked.

His wife called their insurance company and the agent explained that if the business was a total loss the insurance was in the amount of $500,000. "Why don't you just go ahead and send us a check for the $500,000 then?" the wife asked.

"We don't actually pay you the money," the agent explained. "We pay to replace the building and the equipment so you end up with something that's equal to the old one. That's how insurance works."

The wife thought a few seconds and said, "If that's how insurance works, then I'd like to cancel the life insurance policy I have on my husband."

....

The wisdom of Richard Branson

Sir Richard Charles Nicholas Branson is an English business magnate and investor. He is best known as the founder of Virgin Group, which is made up of more than four hundred companies.

His first business venture was a magazine called *The Student* at the age of 16. Branson advertised popular records in *The Student* and the business was an overnight success.

In 1970, started his record business from the crypt of a church where he ran the magazine. Trading under the name "Virgin," he sold records for considerably less than popular retail outlets.

Branson is the fourth richest citizen of the U.K., according to the *Forbes* 2012 list of billionaires, with an estimated net worth of US$4.6 billion.

Some of his wisdom...

"With the casino and the beds, our passengers will have at least two ways to get lucky on one of our flights."

"I find it impossible to stop my brain from churning through all the ideas and possibilities facing me at any given moment."

"I wanted to be an editor or a journalist, I wasn't really interested in being an entrepreneur, but I soon found I had to become an entrepreneur in order to keep my magazine going."

"I never get the accountants in before I start up a business. It's done on gut feeling, especially if I can see that they are taking the mickey out of the consumer."

"A business has to be involving, it has to be fun, and it has to exercise your creative instincts."

"Ridiculous yachts and private planes and big limousines won't make people enjoy life more, and it sends out terrible messages to the people who work for them. It would be so much better if that money was spent in Africa – and it's about getting a balance."

More amazingly wrong predictions

"Computers in the future may weigh no more than 1-1/2 tons."
Popular Mechanics *magazine, forecasting the Future of science in 1949*

"There is no reason for any individual to have a computer in his home."
Ken Olsen, US executive, President of Digital Equipment

"We don't like their sound, and guitar music is on the way out." *Decca Recording Co., regarding the Beatles in 1962*

"Stocks have reached what looks like a permanently high plateau."
Irving Fisher, noted economist of the time, just three days before the 1929 market crash

In the 1999 book *Dow 36,000: The New Strategy for Profiting from the Coming Rise in the Stock*

Market, authors James Glassman and Kevin Hassett claimed that boom times would cause the Dow Jones Industrial Average to rise to 36,000 within just a few years.

"Remote shopping, while entirely feasible, will flop - because women like to get out of the house, like to handle merchandise, like to be able to change their minds."
Time *magazine made this prediction in 1966*

"Television won't be able to hold onto any market it captures after the first six months. People will soon get tired of staring at a plywood box every night." *Darryl F. Zanuck in 1946*

A dedicated manager

A sales rep, an admin, and their manager are walking to lunch when they pass an antique store with an oil lamp in the window. They look at each other and all have the same idea. They enter the store, grab the lamp and rub it. A Genie comes out in a puff of smoke. The Genie says, "I only grant three wishes, so I'll give each of you one wish."

"Let me wish first!" says the admin. "I want to be in the Bahamas, sailing a boat, without a care in the world!"

Within an instant – Poof! She's gone.

The sales rep says, "Me next! Me next! I want to be in Hawaii, relaxing on the beach with my personal masseuse, an endless supply of tropical drinks and the love of my life."

Poof! And the sales person is gone.

"OK, you're up," the Genie says to the manager.

The manager says, "I want those two back in the office right after lunch."

Ideas for Better Business

What's your "Trojan horse" message?

In his book *Contagious: Why Things Catch On*, Jonah Berger explains that a "Trojan horse message" is a fascinating, enthralling narrative that carries a marketing message inside.

Consumers and business decision makers in today's world are overwhelmed with a never-ending stream of marketing communication. Besides media ads, billboards, direct mail and other traditional messages, new electronic marketing techniques have added exponentially to the communication logjam. That makes the task of getting through the communication clutter more difficult than it has ever been.

Enveloping your selling message in a compelling story is an effective way to stand out in the communication clutter. The best Trojan horse stories are those that don't reveal the marketing message until near the end, but when it is revealed, the sales message is so relevant to the story that listeners or viewers can't help but come away with a memorable association that will stick with them.

Trojan horses can be brief stories that fit within the confines of a 30-second commercial, a lengthy posting in a blog, or anywhere in between.

The wisdom of Henry Ford

Henry Ford was an American industrialist and the founder of the Ford Motor Company. Henry Ford did not invent the automobile, but he developed and manufactured the first automobile that many middle class Americans could afford to buy. His introduction of the Model T revolutionized transportation and American industry. As owner of the Ford Motor Company, he became one of the richest people in the world. He is credited with pioneering the mass production of inexpensive goods coupled with high wages for workers. His intense commitment to systematically lowering costs resulted in many technical and business innovations, including a franchise system that put dealerships throughout most of North America and in major cities on six continents.

Some of Henry Ford's wisdom...

"Make the best quality goods possible at the lowest cost possible, paying the highest wages possible."

"Don't find fault, find a remedy."

"Failure is simply the opportunity to begin again, this time more intelligently."

"Employers only handle the money – it is the customer who pays the wages."

"Thinking is the hardest work there is, which is probably the reason so few engage in it."

"The only real mistake is the one from which we learn nothing."

"If I had asked people what they wanted, they would have said 'faster horses.'"

"If there is any one secret of success, it lies in the ability to get the other person's point of view and see things from that person's angle as well as from your own."

"Vision without execution is just hallucination."

"There is no man living who isn't capable of doing more than he thinks he can do."

"A business that makes nothing but money is a poor business."

"You don't have to hold a position in order to be a leader."

"Quality means doing it right when no one is looking."

"To do more for the world than the world does for you – that is success."

Ideas for Better Business

Five tips for small business success

A business doesn't have to be a giant multinational corporation to follow good business practices. In fact, some of the best businesses have evolved and grown by implementing some of these principles.

Know-how is not enough

Being an expert in a particular field doesn't guarantee success. Almost all small businesses need marketing savvy and administration skills (at the very least) to get the enterprise off the ground.

One of the most common explanations for a failed small business is that the owners were not organized in the administrative end of the business.

Many community colleges and tech schools offer courses in small business management that may be helpful in building a complete skill set needed for business success.

Hire the right people

The "I can do it all" entrepreneur often runs into roadblocks. It is a valuable exercise to do an honest and thorough analysis of personal strengths and weaknesses, and then plan to hire the right people to fill in the blanks.

Don't make snap decisions

In the hectic world of an entrepreneur who wears multiple hats and is constantly pressed for time, it's tempting to skip over analysis and make decisions solely from the gut. While instincts should not be completely ignored, if a small business owner habitually makes decisions in haste, eventually they will make a terrible one.

Promoting from within can be a wise move...or a huge mistake

Promoting from within encourages self-development and gives a goal to some staff members. But a small business manager must constantly be on the lookout for talent and skills that complement their own and improve the company's overall level of competence. Sometimes that person is already on the team...but sometimes it's better to look outside.

Good business is the result of consistency

McDonald's pioneered and epitomizes this idea. When customers walk into a McDonald's anywhere in the United States, they know exactly what to expect – right down to the exact ingredients, quantities, and even the order of toppings. Consistency literally screams to customers, "This business is well managed and professional!"

Quotes about rising from adversity

"What does not destroy me, makes me stronger." – *Friedrich Nietzsche*

"Great works are performed not by strength but by perseverance." – *Samuel Johnson*

"He knows not his own strength that hath not met adversity." – *Ben Jonson*

"When it's darkest, men see the stars."
- *Ralph Waldo Emerson*

"Success is how high you bounce when you hit bottom." – *General George S. Patton*

"When the well's dry, we know the worth of water." – *Benjamin Franklin*

"A certain amount of opposition is a great help to a man. Kites rise against, not with the wind."
– *John Neal*

"Life is not always a matter of holding good cards, but sometimes playing a poor hand well."
– *Jack London*

Bone-headed business blunders quiz

What chocolate company passed on a movie tie-in that resulted in an estimated $20 million of free publicity for a competitor? What was the movie? What product ended up reaping the rewards?

What over-the-counter product's market share dropped from 37% to 7% overnight after a tampering scare in 1982? (Extra credit for knowing what major city the scare originated in)

What company's President wrote Alexander Graham Bell in 1876 to tell him that his invention "was an interesting novelty but had no commercial possibilities"?

Answers to bone-headed business blunders

Mars was approached by the producers of *E.T. The Extra Terrestrial* to use M&M's in the film. They passed, and Hershey's used the movie to launch their new candy brand, Reese's Pieces, which became an overnight success.

While the event caused a large dip in sales, Johnson & Johnson's handling of the "Tylenol scare" was hardly a blunder. The company recalled 100 million bottles and redesigned the packaging with three layers of tamper-proofing. After the initial plunge in market share following the tampering incidents in Chicago, the brand bounced back and Johnson & Johnson became a positive case study subject for how to handle crisis public relations.

Western Union President William Orton passed on Alexander Graham Bell's invention, the telephone.

● ●

Quotes about risk taking

"Security is mostly a superstition. Life is either a daring adventure or nothing." - *Helen Keller*

"Do not fear mistakes. There are none."
- *Miles Davis*

"Give me the young man who has brains enough to make a fool of himself."
- *Robert Louis Stevenson*

"Whatever you can do, or dream you can do, you should begin it. Boldness has genius, power and magic in it." - *Goethe*

"Ninety-nine percent of success is built on failure."
- *Charles Kettering*

● ●

● ●

"No matter how well you perform, there's always somebody of intelligent opinion who thinks it's lousy." *- Sir Laurence Olivier*

"You must do the thing you think you cannot do." *- Eleanor Roosevelt*

"You miss one-hundred percent of the shots you never take." *- Wayne Gretzky*

"The man with a new idea is a crank - until the idea succeeds." *- Mark Twain*

"I failed my way to success." *- Thomas Edison*

"Too many of us are not living our dreams because we are living our fears." *- Les Brown*

● ●

"Because you were a gentleman."

One of the biggest journalism coups of the last century happened when *Life* magazine secured the rights to the "Zapruder film," which was the best video record of the Kennedy assassination.

Los Angeles bureau chief Dick Stolley of *Life* received a tip from the correspondent in Dallas that a local businessman named Abraham Zapruder had captured the assassination on film. Stolley flew to Dallas and immediately began calling Zapruder's home, but there was no answer because the photographer was driving around Dallas in a frantic search for someone who would develop his movie that same night.

Finally at 11 p.m. Zapruder answered his phone. Stolley initially pushed for a meeting that same night, but Zapruder seemed very weary and Stolley decided to back off. Zapruder suggested they meet in his office at 9 a.m. the next morning. Stolley showed up an hour early and was able to view the film as Zapruder screened it for two Secret Service agents.

Just as he was about to talk about making a deal with Zapruder, the office was flooded with competitors who also wanted to buy the rights to the film.

While Zapruder screened the film for the other journalists, Stolley sat in the office and visited with Zapruder's staff. In particular, he connected with Zapruder's secretary, who grew up in the same part of the Midwest as Stolley.

After the screenings, Zapruder announced that since Stolley had contacted him first, he would have the first chance to bid on the film.

The other reporters howled in anger as Stolley and Zapruder walked into the private office and closed the door. Their discussion was frequently interrupted by loud pounding on the door, shouting, and notes constantly being slid underneath. Zapruder could hear his secretary being badgered rudely by reporters while she protected the entrance to his inner sanctum.

As they talked, Stolley quietly and politely addressed Zapruder's concerns, especially stressing that *Life* would not exploit the film in any way. Stolley remained calm as Zapruder's asking price continued to rise, but at the $50,000 mark he announced that his bosses would have to approve anything greater than that amount.

(continued on next page)

(continued from previous page)

At that point, Zapruder simply said, "Let's do it," and signed the contract for $50,000. *Life* editors followed up two days later and added an additional $100,000 for television rights.

For years after, Dick Stolley wondered why Zapruder signed the deal so quickly with him, rather than turn the film's sale into a bidding war, which almost certainly would have netted him a higher price. Long after Zapruder passed away in 1970, Stolley had occasion to speak to Zapruder's long-time business partner, who asked him, "Do you know why you got that film instead of the other reporters?"

"Why?" Stolley asked.

"Because you were a gentleman," he answered.

Origin of the legal pad

Most historians believe that the legal pad got its start with Thomas Holley in 1888. Holley was a worker at a paper mill in Massachusetts. He noted that the company threw out a lot of scrap pieces, called sortings, left over from cutting paper into the right sized sheets. He daydreamed about how there might be a use for them, and eventually thought of cutting the sortings to the same size and binding them into small notepads. Since the paper was going to be thrown out otherwise, the mill could sell the pads at low prices.

The first few batches of pads sold very well, and Holley quit his job to start his own company, collecting scraps from the local mills and manufacturing them into pads.

The pads that Holley made weren't yellow. The origin of the use of yellow color is not clear. Holley's initial pads were white, and making them yellow would have increased his costs and ruined his business plan. Office product history buffs believe that yellow was adopted as a standard color because it contrasted well against black or blue ink without glare, making text easier to read.

━ ‥ ━ ‥ ━ ‥ ━ ‥ ━ ‥ ━ ‥ ━ ‥

Fascinating quotes

"A problem well stated is a problem half solved."
- Charles Kettering

"Don't be afraid to take a big step when it is indicated. You can't cross a chasm in two small jumps." *- David Lloyd George*

"You will never find the time for anything. If you want time, you must make it." *- Charles Burton*

"One of the illusions of life is that the present hour is not the critical, decisive one."
- Ralph Waldo Emerson

"Nothing is more dangerous than an idea when it is the only one you have." *- Emile Chartier*

━ ‥ ━ ‥ ━ ‥ ━ ‥ ━ ‥ ━ ‥ ━ ‥

▬ ∙ ∙ ▬ ∙ ∙ ▬ ∙ ∙ ▬ ∙ ∙ ▬ ∙ ∙ ▬ ∙

"Our best ideas come from clerks and stock boys."
- *Sam Walton*

"Time flies like an arrow. Fruit flies like a banana."
- *Groucho Marx*

"Imagination is more important than knowledge."
- *Albert Einstein*

"If you go to your grave without painting your masterpiece, it will not get painted. No one else can paint it." - *Gordon MacKenzie*

"You can have brilliant ideas, but if you can't get them across, your ideas won't get you anywhere."
- *Lee Iaccocca*

▬ ∙ ∙ ▬ ∙ ∙ ▬ ∙ ∙ ▬ ∙ ∙ ▬ ∙ ∙ ▬ ∙

Secrets behind the giant union rat

If you live in a major city on the East Coast, you probably have seen the giant rat balloons that unions use to protest companies using non-union labor.

"Scabby," the giant union rat was created by Big Sky Balloons and Searchlights in 1990, at the request of the Chicago Bricklayers Union. Big Sky owner Mike O'Connor sketched several versions of the rat until the union approved the final design as being "mean-looking enough."

The idea quickly caught on with other unions. The rat business began booming and Big Sky received orders from all over the country. Most of the rats went to New York City, and soon there were at least thirty giant rat balloons in the New York metro area.

Even today, Big Sky sells as many as two hundred rats a year, ranging from the compact 6-foot model (cost is approximately $2,000) to the really giant 25-foot rodent (cost is about $8,000). The most popular size is the intermediate 12-foot model, which fits standing up in the back of a pickup and gets attention without breaking standard ordinances that limit the height of inflatable displays.

In 2011, Federal regulators ruled that union activists have the legal right to display the rats outside of companies during labor disputes. The New Jersey state Supreme Court similarly ruled in 2011 that the use of the rats in labor protests is protected speech under the First Amendment, overturning a township ordinance that banned any inflatable signs not being used for a store's grand opening.

Surprising celebrity business ventures

Can you match the business venture with the celebrity? (Answers follow)

Business venture:

1. Product licensing

2. Salad dressing

3. Pro football team

4. Wigs

5. Stripper poles

6. Bakery/deli

7. Organic snacks

8. Vegan shoes

9. Comic book store

10. Environmental clean-up systems

11. Wine

Celebrity:

A. Carmen Electra

B. Elizabeth Hurley

C. Sandra Bullock

D. Francis Ford Coppola

E. Natalie Portman

F. Donald Trump

E. Kathy Ireland

F. Kevin Costner

G. Raquel Welch

H. Paul Newman

I. Kevin Smith

Answers to celebrity business ventures

1. Product licensing - E. Kathy Ireland. She holds a ten-percent stake in Kathy Ireland Worldwide, a $1.5 billion licensing business

2. Salad dressing - H. Paul Newman – In 1982, Newman introduced a line of salad dressings, which have since expanded into coffee, condiments, sauces and other foods. The company has donated over $380 million to charity since its inception.

3. Pro football team - F. Donald Trump – Trump owned the New Jersey Generals of the ill-fated United States Football League. The league was initially set up to play during the NFL off-season and use players from colleges surrounding each team's city, but Trump's insistence on competing head-to-head with the NFL doomed the league after only a few seasons.

4. Wigs - G. Raquel Welch – Her company's name is HairUWear

5. Stripper poles - A. Carmen Electra – Her company sells stripper poles as well as instructional videos

6. Bakery/deli - C. Sandra Bullock – Walton's Fancy & Staple is located in Austin, Texas

7. Organic snacks - B. Elizabeth Hurley - Her line is sold exclusively at Harrod's in London

8. Vegan shoes - E. Natalie Portman – Her non-leather shoes are sold at her boutique, Te Casan in New York

9. Comic book store - I. Kevin Smith – Smith purchased a store in Red Bank, NJ and changed the name to "Jay & Silent Bob's Secret Stash"

10. Environmental clean-up systems - F. Kevin Costner – Ocean Therapy Solutions was acquired by Costner in 1995

11. Wine - D. Francis Ford Coppola – He acquired a California winery in 1975 and changed the label to his own name

Business ideas to use

Presentation flubs and how to avoid them

Everyone in business has been there at least once - standing in front of the room, lights dimmed, and the opening PowerPoint slide shining brightly on the screen. People are paying attention and taking notes. Then disaster strikes.

Any number of things can derail a presentation. Some are out of the presenter's control, but many can be avoided. Here are some mistakes to avoid:

Lack of confidence by the presenter – The worst thing a presenter can lead off with is an excuse. Saying something like, "Sorry, but I didn't find out about this until yesterday so I haven't had much time to prepare" is a sure way to lose the audience from the start.

Typos or incorrect figures – Years ago, I made an ad campaign pitch to a committee and didn't double-check the math on one of the pages of the handout. The presentation was limited to twenty minutes, about fifteen of which were spent explaining the error and what the correct number should have been.

Getting off track – Presenters can't expect to follow their presentations exactly. Stuff happens. But when questions arise or one slide triggers an intense discussion, it is up to the presenter to bring the audience back and return the focus to the presentation. If the discussion has gone so far off track that people start checking their email, it's time to take back control.

"Your probably can't read this, but…" – Putting up data or text that the audience can't read from the farthest reaches of the room is the kiss of death when it comes to capturing the audience. Never, ever show a slide that no one can read. If necessary, break up the slide into two or more slides.

The way to prevent these flubs is simple: Prepare, prepare, prepare.

Practice your presentation several times. Make sure all the data presented are right. Be in charge of the room. Try to show pictures, not data that is impossible to read. If you must use data, break it down so it's large on the screen.

More thoughts about success

"If I told you I've worked hard to get where I'm at, I'd be lying, because I have no idea where I am right now." — *Jarod Kintz, This Book is Not for Sale*

"It had long since come to my attention that people of accomplishment rarely sat back and let things happen to them. They went out and happened to things." — *Leonardo da Vinci*

"A thinker sees his own actions as experiments and questions – as attempts to find out something. Success and failure are for him answers above all." — *Friedrich Nietzsche*

"In order to succeed, your desire for success should be greater than your fear of failure." — *Bill Cosby*

"If you don't build your dream, someone else will hire you to help them build theirs." – *Dhirubhai Ambani*

Thinking on one's feet

The CEO of a major company, who had a reputation for being brusque, stopped for a quick lunch at an upscale restaurant where he was a well-known regular. Since he wasn't too hungry, he asked the waiter for half of a sirloin steak.

Normally the waiter would simply have refused the request, since the restaurant didn't serve half steaks. But given the importance of this particular customer, the waiter agreed to the unusual request and walked toward the kitchen to put in the order.

Unbeknownst to the waiter, the CEO had followed him to the kitchen to remind him that he wanted the steak cooked rare. As the waiter announced to the chef, "I need half a steak for a real jerk," he noticed out of the corner of his eye the customer standing behind him and without missing a beat added, "and the other half goes to this gentleman."

The wisdom of Roger Sterling

Roger H. Sterling, Jr., played by John Slattery, is a fictional character on the AMC TV series *Mad Men*. After serving in WWII, Roger Sterling  started his career working for Sterling Cooper, an advertising agency in New York City that his father co-founded, and later became a founding partner at the newly formed advertising firm of Sterling Cooper Draper Pryce in late 1963.

Sterling was a notorious womanizer and a heavy drinker (he described himself as "living like he was on shore leave") until two heart attacks changed his perspective, at least temporarily. However, his health scares did not permanently curtail his drinking or smoking habits.

Some of Roger Sterling's wisdom...

"I'll tell you what brilliance in advertising is: Ninety-nine cents. Somebody thought of that."

"Half the time, this business comes down to: 'I don't like that guy.'"

"I shall be both dog and pony."

"The day you sign a client is the day you start losing them."

"I'm being punished for making my job look easy."

"Have a drink. It'll make me look younger."

"It looks like you're all going to engage in a little mid-level camaraderie, so I'll be on my way."

"I never get used to the fact that most of the time it looks like you're doing nothing."

"Your loyalty is starting to become a liability."

"Every generation thinks the next one is the end of it all. I bet there were people in the Bible walking around, complaining about 'kids today.'"

Quotes compiled from the book *Sterling's Gold: Wit & Wisdom of an Ad Man*, Lion's Gate Television

· ·

"Pound the rock"

When Jon Gruden became coach of the Tampa
Bay Buccaneers, his challenge was to instill a work
ethic and winning attitude into an organization
that had a history of mediocrity. Gruden was convinced that the talent was in place to win a cham-
pionship, but the team needed a unifying philoso-
phy.

Gruden came up with the mantra for the 2002
season which he called, "pound the rock." The
saying was meant to drive home the idea of working toward a goal, each and every day. At first, the
goal seems impossible, but he convinced the organization that if everyone "pounded the rock"
each and every day, eventually the seemingly impossible goal of breaking the rock could be
achieved.

To make the point, Gruden had a giant granite
boulder installed near the team entrance. Each
day, the players would pass the rock and hit it, a
daily reminder that the hard work they put in each
day at practice might not bring results immediately but would eventually pay off. The motiva-

· ·

•••••••••••••••••••••••••••••••

tional strategy was a key factor in Tampa Bay dominating the NFL that season and eventually winning Super Bowl XXXVII. Upon returning to Tampa after winning the Super Bowl, Jon Gruden led a capacity crowd at Tampa Bay's Raymond James Stadium in chanting the phrase.

Later, the Jacksonville Jaguars attempted the idea with disastrous results. Their slogan, "Keep chopping wood," involved players picking up an axe and hitting a huge log in the player entrance. Unfortunately, punter Chris Hanson injured his leg with the axe and as a result of the injury was placed on injured reserve. The idea never had the impact of Gruden's brainstorm.

•••••••••••••••••••••••••••••••

More on consultants

The American and the Chinese corporate offices
for a multi-national corporation decided to engage
in a competitive boat race, and both practiced hard
in order to reach their peak performance.

On race day they felt ready. The Chinese team won
easily. Afterward, the discouraged American team
decided that the reason for the crushing defeat
had to be found, so a consulting firm was hired to
investigate the problem and recommended correc-
tive action.

The consultant's finding: The Chinese team had
eight people rowing and one person steering; the
American team had one person rowing and eight
people steering.

So, as race day approached again the following
year, the consultant recommended a complete re-
structure of the American team's management.
The new structure: four steering managers, three
area steering managers and a performance review
system for the person rowing the boat in order to
provide work incentive.

The next year, the Chinese won by even more. Hu-
miliated, the consultant recommended that the
rower be terminated for poor performance and
charged an extra fee for discovering the problem.

Know your business buzzwords

The Cloud – remote servers that store applications and files that were traditionally stored in a local device like a PC or tablet

Game changer – an event or strategy that significantly alters the competitive landscape

YOLO – you only live once as in "Bro, come out for a beer after work, YOLO."

Value proposition – the benefits that make your product or service worth the asking price

Hard stop – pretentious phrase for a definitive cut-off time, as in, "I can only talk for 10 minutes, I have a 10:45 hard stop."

(continued on following page)

(Business buzzwords, continued)

Manage expectations – explaining in advance to a superior or a customer why they are not getting what they thought they would be getting

Hit the slide – to quit a job in spectacular fashion

Scooby snacks – low cost tokens given as rewards to employees, as in "Now that he's dead, Joe's ergonomic chair is available, so go ahead and take it."

'trep – pretentious shorthand for entrepreneur

Osmosis marketing – brand success achieved by online buzz and word of mouth instead of traditional marketing methods

Ramen profitable – derogatory term for a business that is eking out small profits

Digital nomad – a worker who has no office or desk, but instead uses wireless technology

Sign wars

When F. W. Woolworth opened his first store, a merchant on the same street tried to undermine the new competitor by hanging out a big sign on his storefront: "Doing business in this same spot for over fifty years." The next day Woolworth also put out a sign. It read: "Established one week ago: our entire stock is brand new!"

•••••••••••••••••••••••••••••••••••••••

Three competing stores were side-by-side on a downtown street. The store owner in the middle felt trouble was brewing when the store to his right put up a huge banner saying, "BEST DEALS ON THE BLOCK!"

The shop owner was even more horrified when the competitor on his left hung an equally large sign, reading "LOWEST PRICES ON THE BLOCK!"

The store owner resisted the urge to panic and instead came up with an idea. He put a huge sign directly over the door to his own store. It read: "MAIN ENTRANCE HERE"

Quotable quotes

"Develop success from failures. Discouragement and failure are two of the surest stepping stones to success." – *Dale Carnegie*

"There are only two ways to live life. One is as though nothing is a miracle. The other is as though everything is." – *Albert Einstein*

"Do not look for approval except for the consciousness of doing your best." – *Andrew Carnegie*

"The true measure of a person is how they treat someone who can do him absolutely no good."
– *Samuel Johnson*

"You've got to be very careful if you don't know where you are going because you might not get there." – *Yogi Berra*

"Expect more than others think possible."
– *Howard Schultz*

"If people aren't calling you crazy, you aren't thinking big enough." – *Richard Branson*

"Never, never, never give up." – *Winston Churchill*

Thoughts on risk taking

"The way to succeed is to double your failure rate." - *Thomas Watson*

"You can only be as good as you dare to be bad." - *John Barrymore*

"No idea is so outlandish that it should not be considered." - *Winston Churchill*

"There's always an element of chance and you must be willing to live with that element. If you insist on certainty, you will paralyze yourself." - *J. Paul Getty*

"Almost all really new ideas have a certain aspect of foolishness when they are just produced." - *A.N. Whitehead*

"Taking a new step, uttering a new word is what people fear most." - *Fyodor Dostoevsky*

"Microsoft is always two years away from failure." - *Bill Gates*

"If I have a thousand ideas and only one turns out to be good, I am satisfied." - *Alfred Nobel*

The wisdom of Mary Kay Ash

Mary Kay Ash left the traditional workplace after watching yet another man whom she had trained get promoted over her. She started her own cosmetics company, and her marketing skills combined with people savvy led her company to enormous success.

Ash wanted everyone in the organization to have the opportunity to benefit from their successes. Sales representatives—Ash called them consultants—bought the products from Mary Kay at wholesale prices and then sold them at retail price to their customers. They could also earn commissions from new consultants that they had recruited.

Today there are more than 1.6 million salespeople working for Mary Kay Inc. around the world.

Some of her wisdom...

"Pretend that every single person you meet has a sign around his or her neck that says, 'Make me feel important.' Not only will you succeed in sales, you will succeed in life."

"Those who are blessed with the most talent don't necessarily outperform everyone else. It's the people with follow-through who excel."

"God didn't have time to make a nobody, only a somebody. I believe that each of us has God-given talents within us waiting to be brought to fruition."

"A mediocre idea that generates enthusiasm will go further than a great idea that inspires no one."

"Sandwich every bit of criticism between two thick layers of praise."

"Don't limit yourself. Many people limit themselves to what they think they can do. You can go as far as your mind lets you. What you believe, remember, you can achieve."

"We must have a theme, a goal, a purpose in our lives. If you don't know where you're aiming, you don't have a goal. My goal is to live my life in such a way that when I die, someone can say, she cared."

"People are definitely a company's greatest asset. It doesn't make any difference whether the product is cars or cosmetics. A company is only as good as the people it keeps."

Salary negotiation

Fresh out of business school, a young man answered an employment listing for an accountant. He was interviewed by an entrepreneur who was proud owner of a one-man small business.

"I need someone with an accounting degree," the man said. "But mainly, I'm looking for someone to take away my money worries."

"Excuse me?" the recently graduate asked.

"I worry about a lot of things," the man said. "But I don't want to have to worry about money. Your job will be to take all the money problems off my back."

"I see," the accountant said. "And how much does the job pay?"

"I'll start you at a hundred thousand."

"A hundred thousand dollars!" the accountant exclaimed. "That's much more than the big accounting firms are paying for a new hire. How can such a small business afford to pay a salary like that?"

"That," the owner said, "is the first thing I want you to figure out."

Business trivia

The idea for the original concept of Netflix was born when Reed Hastings was fined $40 for a late return of the video *Apollo 13*.

—··—··—··—··—··

In 2012, the BBC came out with a list of the largest employers in the world. Topping the list was the United States Department of Defense, with 3.2 million people. Second and third were the People's Liberation Army of China (2.3 million) and Wal-Mart (2.1 million).

—··—··—··—··—··

Coca-Cola announced a few years ago that they would resume business operations in Burma/Myanmar after a sixty year absence. Since then, there are only two countries in the entire world where Coca-Cola has no business presence: North Korea and Cuba.

—··—··—··—··—··

One of the largest downfalls in business history is Kodak. As recently as the late 1990's, Kodak appeared in the top five of several published lists of the most valuable brands. In 1976 the company had a 90% market share of photographic film sales in the United States. However, 2007 was the most recent year in which the company made a profit and the company declared bankruptcy in 2012.

It's a small world

Two women are playing a round of golf, and they are holding up the two business men playing behind them.

After about four holes, one of the executives says to the other, "I'm going to go ask them if they don't mind letting us play through."

But as the man approaches the women, he suddenly changes his mind and walks back to his fellow golfer.

"What's the problem?" his golfing buddy asks.

The man, who now has turned pale, answers, "There's no way I can talk to them. One is my wife, and the other one is my mistress."

The golfing buddy snorts and says, "I'm not afraid to ask them!" He walks toward the women but just as suddenly as his friend, he turns around and walks straight back.

"I can't talk to them either," he says.

"What's your problem talking to them?"

His friend grins sheepishly and simply says, "Small world isn't it?"

Business school trivia

1. Which university's business school offered MBA classes via closed-circuit television in 1961, long before remote classrooms were widely used?

2. Which business school was the first to host an "electronic computer," the IBM 650, in 1955?

3. Which business school is housed in a building named after Houston Texans owner Bob McNair and his wife Janice?

4. Which university's business school has built at least ten Habitat for Humanity houses?

5. In a 25 year-old tradition at this business school, students participate in the "Beer Games," a business simulation involving a fictional beer company but no actual beer.

6. Staying with the beer theme, which business school's building was christened with a bottle of Heineken when it opened in 1993?

7. This business school was established in 1935 as the College of Business Administration; its curriculum focused typing, auctioneering, and shorthand.

8. Which business school has twelve alumni who went on to become deans of business schools?

Answers:

1. Indiana University

2. Carnegie Mellon University's school of business

3. Rice University's Jones Graduate School of Business

4. The University of North Carolina at Chapel Hill

5. MIT's Sloan School of Management

6. The University of Maryland's Smith School of Business. At the time, Leo Van Munching Jr., a graduate for whom the hall is named, was president of the company holding the U.S. rights to import and distribute Heineken beer.

7. UCLA's Anderson School of Management

8. University of California at Berkeley's Haas School of Business

Business quotes

"If you owe the bank $100, that's your problem. If you owe the bank $100 million, that's the bank's problem." - *J. Paul Getty*

"Success and failure are both difficult to endure. Along with success come drugs, divorce, fornication, bullying, travel, medication, depression, neurosis and suicide. With failure comes failure."
- *Joseph Heller*

"By working faithfully eight hours a day you may eventually get to be boss and work twelve hours a day." - *Robert Frost*

"Accomplishing the impossible means only the boss will add it to your regular duties."
- *Doug Larson*

— — — — — — — — — — — — — — — ▪

"If you can count your money, you don't have a billion dollars." - *J. Paul Getty*

"Don't stay in bed, unless you can make money in bed." - *George Burns*

"When in doubt, route." - *Malcolm S. Forbes*

"The best way to appreciate your job is to imagine yourself without one." - *Oscar Wilde*

"One of the symptoms of an approaching nervous breakdown is the belief that one's work is terribly important." - *Bertrand Russell*

"Never interrupt your enemy when he is making a mistake." - *Napoleon Bonaparte*

— — — — — — — — — — — — — — — ▪

Government at work

Scientists for an auto and truck manufacturer developed an invention to simulate high speed collisions with flocks of birds in order to test the strength of their windshields. It was a gun built to propel whole chickens at the windshields of cars and trucks. One of the cleverest things about the gun was that it used chickens that were readily available at the nearest grocery store.

Government engineers heard about the invention and were eager to use it to test the windshields of their military planes. Arrangements were made, and when the gun was fired, the government engineers were shocked to see the chicken hurtle out of the barrel, crash right through the shatterproof windshield and embed itself in the back of the pilot's cockpit seat.

Horrified, the government engineers sent their counterparts at the car maker videos of the disastrous tests and begged the car company for suggestions.

The car company's engineers had a short response that said, "THAW THE CHICKEN FIRST!"

Overheard in a job interview…

Employer: "For this job, it's vitally important that we have someone who is responsible."

Applicant: "Then I'm perfect for the position. On my last job, every time anything went wrong, they said I was responsible."

***

Applicant, as he answers cell phone in middle of interview: "I have to take this call…would you mind stepping out for a few minutes? It's a private conversation."

***

Employer: "How long do you expect to stay in this position?"

Applicant: "Probably not too long. I'm looking at a pretty big inheritance if my uncle dies, and he isn't looking too good."

***

Employer: "Why did you leave your last job?"

Applicant: "I was fired for beating up my boss."

━ ▪ ━ ▪ ━ ▪ ━ ▪ ━ ▪ ━ ▪

The four envelopes

A new manager crossed paths with the manager he was replacing. As he was leaving, the outgoing manager said to him, "I'm going to do you a big favor. I left four numbered envelopes in the desk drawer. The first time you encounter a crisis you can't solve, open envelope number one. When the second crisis hits, open the second envelope, and so on."

A couple of months down the road there was a major crisis where everything seemed to be going wrong. The new manager remembered the parting words of his predecessor and opened the first envelope. The message inside said, "Blame your predecessor!" The new manager convinced everyone that the problem was caused by his predecessor and was off the hook.

Another few months passed and the company experienced plunging sales. The manager quickly opened the second envelope, and it said simply, "Blame the economy!" The manager compiled economic data and upper management reluctantly agreed the economy was perhaps to blame, and the manager was once again spared.

━ ▪ ━ ▪ ━ ▪ ━ ▪ ━ ▪ ━ ▪

━ ▪ ━ ▪ ━ ▪ ━ ▪ ━ ▪ ━ ▪ ▪

Later that same year, major product defects arose and forced a recall. This time, envelope number three gave the advice, "Reorganize!" The manager did so, and the company rebounded.

An entire year passed and things seemed to be going smoothly, but suddenly another major crisis erupted, this one even more dire and job-threatening than the first three. The manager decided he must open the fourth envelope. The message inside said, "Prepare four envelopes."

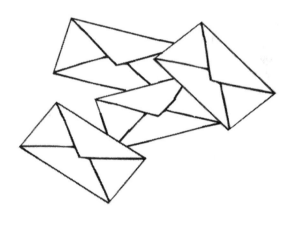

━ ▪ ━ ▪ ━ ▪ ━ ▪ ━ ▪ ━ ▪ ▪

The wisdom of Michael Eisner

Michael Eisner was born into a family of successful business people. His mother's family founded the American Safety Razor Company, his father was a successful lawyer and administrator, his great-grandfather established a clothing company that was one of the first uniform suppliers to the Boy Scouts of America, and his great-grandmother belonged to an immigrant family that established the town of Red Bank, New Jersey.

After two brief stints at NBC and CBS, Eisner became Assistant to the National Programming Director at ABC. He moved up the ranks, eventually becoming a senior vice president in charge of programming and development and later the CEO at Paramount Pictures. During his eight-year tenure at Paramount, the studio turned out such memorable films as *Saturday Night Fever* and *Raiders of the Lost Ark*, as well as TV shows including *Happy Days* and *Cheers*.

Eisner became CEO and Chairman of the Board at The Walt Disney Company in 1984. During the second half of the 1980's and early 1990's, Disney was revitalized. Beginning with the films *Who Framed Roger Rabbit* and *The Little Mermaid*, the studio's flagship animation studio enjoyed a series of commercial and critical successes.

The College of Education at California State University Northridge is named in his honor and he was inducted into the Television Academy Hall of Fame in 2012.

Some of his wisdom...

"There's no good idea that can't be improved on."

"In every business, in every industry, management does matter."

"I gravitate toward the team thing. I'm not a golfer - I much prefer basketball."

"If it's not growing, it's going to die."

"My strength is coming up with two outs in the last of the ninth."

"Succeeding is not really a life experience that does that much good. Failing is a much more sobering and enlightening experience."

"When you're trying to create things that are new, you have to be prepared to be on the edge of risk."

"It is rare to find a business partner who is selfless. If you are lucky it happens once in a lifetime."

Thoughts about reputation

"When a management with a reputation for brilliance tackles a business with a reputation for bad economics, it is the reputation of the business that remains intact." - *Warren Buffett*

"A reputation for a thousand years may depend upon the conduct of a single moment."
- *Ernest Bramah*

"A reputation once broken may possibly be repaired, but the world will always keep their eyes on the spot where the crack was." - *Joseph Hall*

"Associate with men of good quality if you esteem your own reputation; for it is better to be alone than in bad company." - *George Washington*

"First, make yourself a reputation for being a creative genius. Second, surround yourself with partners who are better than you are. Third, leave them to get on with it." - *David Ogilvy*

"It takes twenty years to build a reputation and five minutes to ruin it. If you think about that, you'll do things differently." - *Warren Buffett*

Defining your goals

A corporate consultant vacationed in a quaint, small Greek seacoast village. One afternoon, he was strolling along the docks when he passed a fisherman who was unloading a large box of fish from his boat. The visiting executive complimented the fisherman on the size and quality of his catch.

"How long did it take you to get all those fish?" he asked the fisherman.

"Not very long," answered the Greek. "Maybe a couple of hours."

"Why didn't you stay out longer and catch more?"

Shrugging, the Greek explained that his day's catch was sufficient to meet his needs, and those of his family.

The consultant asked, "If you only work a couple hours a day, what do you do with the rest of your time?"

"I sleep late, and then fish a little. I get home in the middle of the afternoon and play with my children, and then I take a nap with my wife. In the evening, I go visit my friends. We dance a little, play the bouzouki, and sing songs. It's a good life."

The consultant said, "I think that I can help you. First

thing, you should be fishing longer every day. That way you'll catch more fish that you can sell, and with the added revenue you can buy a bigger boat. With the cash a larger boat will bring you, you can buy a second boat and a third one, and so on, until you have an entire fleet! Then, instead of selling your fish to a middleman, you can negotiate directly with the fish processors and eventually open your own processing plant."

The fisherman listened intently, staring at the young man.

The man continued, "Just think! You can ship fish to markets all around the world. Eventually, you can move to New York City to manage your huge enter-prise."

"How long will all of this take?" asked the fisherman.

"Perhaps twenty-five years," replied the executive.

"And what will I do after that?" the Greek asked.

"When your business gets really big, you can have an IPO, issue stock and make millions!" exclaimed the consultant with zeal. "Then you'll be able to retire. You can live in a small village near the coast, sleep late, fish for a couple of hours, play with your chil-dren, take a nap with your wife, and spend your eve-nings singing, dancing, and playing the bouzouki with your friends."

More government at work

Three young boys were arguing over which one's father was the fastest. The first boy bragged, "My father is so fast, he can shoot an arrow and then run so fast he passes the target before the arrow gets there!"

The second one counters that claim with, "My father is even faster! He goes to the gun range, shoots a rifle and then can run faster than the bullet!"

The third boy, who has sat smugly though the boasting, finally speaks up and says, "You two don't know the first thing about what speed is. My father works for the City and doesn't end work until 5:00 pm, but he's home by 3:45 every day!"

Quotable quotes

"When we own portions of outstanding businesses with outstanding management, our favorite holding period is forever." - *Warren Buffet*

"Whenever there is a hard job to be done I assign it to a lazy man; he is sure to find an easy way of doing it." - *Walter Chrysler*

"If we allow the celebrity rock-star model of leadership to triumph, we will see the decline of corporations and institutions of all types." - *Jim Collins*

"I think the most important CEO task is defining the course that the business will take over the next five or so years. You have to have the ability to see what the business environment might be like a long way out, not just over the coming months. You need to be able to both set a broad direction, and also to take particular decisions along the way that make that broad direction unfold correctly."
- *Chris Corrigan*

The wisdom of Phil Knight

Philip Hampson "Phil" Knight is an American business magnate and philanthropist. He is the co-founder and chairman of Nike, Inc. and previously served as the chief executive officer of Nike.

A graduate of the University of Oregon and Stanford Graduate School of Business, Knight has donated hundreds of millions of dollars to both schools. He competed on the track team coached by Bill Bowerman at the University of Oregon, with whom he would later co-found Nike.

Knight took a trip around the world after receiving an MBA from Stanford, during which he made a stop in Japan and discovered Tiger-brand running shoes. He was so impressed with the quality and low cost that he made a cold call on the company's president and secured distribution rights for the western United States.

When Knight received shoe samples from the company, he mailed two pairs to his former track coach, hoping to gain a sale and an influential endorsement. To Knight's surprise, Bowerman not only ordered the Tiger shoes but also offered to become a partner with Knight and to provide some design ideas for better running shoes. The two men agreed to a partnership and created Blue Ribbon Sports, forerunner to Nike.

Some of Phil Knight's wisdom…

"There is an immutable conflict at work in life and in business, a constant battle between peace and chaos. Neither can be mastered, but both can be influenced. How you go about that is the key to success."

"We wanted Nike to be the world's best sports and fitness company. Once you say that, you have a focus. You don't end up making wing tips or sponsoring the next Rolling Stones world tour."

"Michael Jordan and Tiger Woods are really part of a very big advertising program, and the fact that they make so much money is because the markets have dictated that they get that money, and the fact that they endorse our products allows us to sell more products and create more jobs."

"The trouble in America is not that we're making too many mistakes, but we are making too few."

"My job is to listen to ideas, maybe cook up a few of my own, and make decisions based on what's good for the shareholders and for the company."

Different Views on Market Potential

Many years ago, two salesmen were sent by a shoe manufacturer to Africa to investigate and report back on market potential.

The first salesman reported back, "There is absolutely no potential here - nobody wears shoes!"

The second salesman reported back, "There is massive potential here - nobody wears shoes!"

Barroom Humor

A salesman, advertising executive, a lawyer and a blonde secretary walk into a bar.

The bartender looks up and says, "Is this some kind of a joke?"

Quotes about success

"The first step toward success is taken when you refuse to be a captive of the environment in which you first find yourself." - *Mark Caine*

"People who succeed have momentum. The more they succeed, the more they want to succeed, and the more they find a way to succeed. Similarly, when someone is failing, the tendency is to get on a downward spiral that can even become a self-fulfilling prophecy." - *Tony Robbins*

"When I dare to be powerful – to use my strength in the service of my vision, then it becomes less and less important whether I am afraid."
- *Audre Lorde*

"Whenever you find yourself on the side of the majority, it is time to pause and reflect."
- *Mark Twain*

"If you don't value your time, neither will others. Stop giving away your time and talents. Value what you know and start charging for it." - *Kim Garst*

"A successful man is one who can lay a firm foundation with the bricks others have thrown at him." - *David Brinkley*

Ideas for better business

Understanding the impact of color

Studies show that the use of color in any sort of communication – whether a presentation, marketing or educational – is a powerful way to enhance effectiveness.

According to the Xerox Corporation:

- A color logo improves brand recognition by 80% versus a black and white logo design

- Messages containing color accents are remembered 39% better

- Comprehension improves by 73% if the content includes color

Colors also generate an emotional response. Some common associations in United States culture include:

- Yellow is often linked with optimism, but loses its effectiveness when over-used

- Red has been shown in studies to stimulate the appetite

- The color white is subliminally connected with truth

- Purple is often associated with sophistication or royalty

- Orange creates an atmosphere of fun and cheerfulness

- Blue is the most popular color not only in the US but worldwide, and is often associated with authority, fiscal responsibility and security

- Green triggers images of health and tranquility

It's important to note that the impact of different colors depends on the culture. The examples above are based on research in the United States, but these same colors may have completely different meanings in other parts of the world.

▬ ‧ ‧ ▬ ‧ ‧ ▬ ‧ ‧ ▬ ‧ ‧ ▬ ‧ ‧

Thoughts on leadership

"Catch someone doing something right."
- Kenneth Blanchard and Spencer Johnson

"Surround yourself with the best people you can find, delegate authority, and don't interfere as long as the policy you've decided upon is being carried out." *- Ronald Reagan*

"A desk is a dangerous place from which to view the world." *- John Le Caré*

"Because a thing seems difficult for you, do not think it impossible for anyone to accomplish."
- Marcus Aurelius

▬ ‧ ‧ ▬ ‧ ‧ ▬ ‧ ‧ ▬ ‧ ‧ ▬ ‧ ‧

━ ·· ━ ·· ━ ·· ━ ·· ━ ··

"Don't equate activity with efficiency. You are paying your key people to see the big picture. Don't let them get bogged down in a lot of meaningless meetings and paper shuffling."
- Harvey Mackay

"Management is efficiency in climbing the ladder of success; leadership determines whether the ladder is leaning against the right wall."
- Stephen R. Covey

"The secret of managing is to keep the guys who hate you away from the guys who are undecided." *-Casey Stengel*

━ ·· ━ ·· ━ ·· ━ ·· ━ ··

Words of wisdom to the new manager

You can't tell which way the train went by looking at the track.

There is no substitute for genuine preparation.

The facts may be interesting but they are often irrelevant.

The careful application of fear is also a form of communication.

Everything should be made as simple as possible, but no simpler.

Friends come and go, but enemies accumulate.

If you think there is good in everybody, you haven't met everybody.

The more you run over a dead cat, the flatter it gets.

This may be as bad as it can get, but don't count on it.

Never wrestle a pig. You both get dirty and the pig likes it.

The wrong way to impress the CEO

A new executive trainee was leaving the office late one evening when he found the CEO standing in front of a paper shredder with a piece of paper in his hand.

"Listen," said the CEO, "this is a very sensitive and important document I have here, and my secretary has left for the night. Can you make this thing work?"

"No problem at all," said the young executive. He turned the machine on, inserted the paper, and pressed the start button.

"Excellent, excellent!" said the CEO as his paper disappeared inside the machine. "I just need one copy."

The wisdom of Andrew Carnegie

Andrew Carnegie was an American industrialist who led the enormous expansion of the American steel industry in the late 19th century. He was also the highest profile philanthropist of his era; his 1889 article *The Gospel of Wealth* called on the rich to use their wealth to improve society, and generated a wave of philanthropy during that period.

Carnegie was born in Scotland and arrived in the United States with his poor parents in 1848. He started as a telegrapher and by the 1860's had investments in railroads, railroad cars, bridges, and oil derricks and accumulated further wealth as a bond salesman. He built the Carnegie Steel Company, which he sold to J.P. Morgan in 1901 for $480 million ($13.5 billion in 2012 Dollars), a transaction that created the U.S. Steel Corporation.

Carnegie devoted the remainder of his life to large-scale philanthropy, with special emphasis on local libraries, world peace, education and scientific research. With his fortune, he built Carnegie Hall and numerous other institutions that bear his name. His life has often been referred to as the classic American "rags to riches" story.

Some of Andrew Carnegie's wisdom...

"Do your duty and a little more and the future will take care of itself."

"There is no class so pitiably wretched as that which possesses money and nothing else."

"I resolved to stop accumulating and begin the infinitely more serious and difficult task of wise distribution."

"I believe the true road to preeminent success in any line is to make yourself master in that line. I have no faith in the policy of scattering one's resources, and in my experience I have rarely if ever met a man who achieved preeminence in money making... who was interested in many concerns. "

"You cannot push anyone up the ladder unless he is willing to climb."

"The man who acquires the ability to take full possession of his own mind may take possession of anything else to which he is justly entitled."

"The average person puts only 25% of his energy and ability into his work. The world takes off its hat to those who put in more than 50% of their capacity, and stands on its head for those few and far between souls who devote 100%."

Great minds speak about management

"Focus on a few key objectives ... I only have three things to do. I have to choose the right people, allocate the right number of dollars, and transmit ideas from one division to another with the speed of light. So I'm really in the business of being the gatekeeper and the transmitter of ideas." - *Jack Welch*

_.._.._.._.._.._.

"Indecision and delays are the parents of failure."
- *George Canning*

_.._.._.._.._.._.

"I just spent six hundred thousand dollars training him. Why would I want anyone else to hire his experience?" - *Thomas Watson, head of IBM, when asked if he was going to fire an executive whose recent mistake cost the company six hundred thousand dollars*

_.._.._.._.._.._.

"Never mistake activity for achievement." - *John Wooden*

_.._.._.._.._.._.

"Worry about being better; bigger will take care of itself. Think one customer at a time and take care of each one the best way you can." - *Gary Comer*

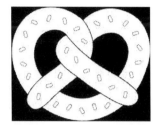

Price increase

There was a pretzel stand in front of an office building in Chicago that sold pretzels for fifty cents each. One day a man exited the building, plunked down two quarters as he passed the pretzel stand and continued walking, without taking a pretzel. This happened every day for two weeks.

Finally, the old lady running the stand stopped him and said, "Sir, excuse me. May I have a word with you?"

The man said: "I know what you're going to say. You're going to ask me why I give you fifty cents every day and don't take a pretzel."

The woman replied, "No, I just wanted to let you know that we raised our price to a dollar."

Thoughts from famous managers

"I'm going to miss Blockbuster. We had an atmosphere where everybody was happy. When people make money, they're happy." - *Wayne Huizenga*

"Management is nothing more than motivating other people." - *Lee Iacocca*

"The people who are doing the work are the moving force behind the Macintosh. My job is to create a space for them, to clear out the rest of the organization and keep it at bay." - *Steve Jobs*

"Go for a business that any idiot can run - because sooner or later, any idiot probably is going to run it." - *Peter Lynch*

"We don't have as many managers as we should, but we would rather have too few than too many." - *Larry Page*

"I have learned the novice can often see things that the expert overlooks. All that is necessary is not to be afraid of making mistakes, or of appearing naive." - *Abraham Maslow*

"Regardless of how well a studio is run, it's only as good as the product it produces."
- *Vince McMahon*

"Understanding how to be a good investor makes you a better business manager and vice versa."
- *Charlie Munger*

"You can't build a strong corporation with a lot of committees and a board that has to be consulted every turn. You have to be able to make decisions on your own." - *Rupert Murdoch*

The wisdom of T. Boone Pickens

Thomas Boone Pickens, Jr. is an American business magnate and financier. Pickens is chairman of the BP Capital Management hedge fund.

At age twelve, Pickens delivered newspapers and quickly expanded his business by acquiring other routes. He later cited his boyhood job as an early introduction to "expanding quickly by acquisition," a business practice he applied later in life.

He graduated with a degree in geology and was hired by Phillips Petroleum, where he worked until 1954. After two years as a wildcatter, he founded the company that later became Mesa Petroleum.

By 1981, Mesa had grown into one of the largest independent oil companies in the world. His corporate acquisitions made him a controversial celebrity during the 1980's to the point where *Time* magazine featured Pickens on the cover for the March 1985 issue.

In recent years he has been an outspoken proponent of energy independence for the US.

Some of his wisdom...

"I say, you work eight hours, and you sleep eight hours - be sure they're not the same eight hours."

"I was very fortunate in my gene mix. The gambling instincts I inherited from my father were matched by my mother's gift for analysis."

"I've always believed that it's important to show a new look periodically. Predictability can lead to failure."

"We've got to move to other sources of energy. But we've gotten way behind, and will continue to pay the fiddler. It's not a good future."

"The older I get, the more I see a straight path where I want to go. If you're going to hunt elephants, don't get off the trail following a rabbit."

"A dollar is not worth as much as you think it is. Your honesty is worth much more."

"I don't go looking for somewhere to spend my money. You can step on a tube of toothpaste for a week, if you have to. I spend what I need to and give it away."

"Given the current state of our finances, we could sure use a quarter of a trillion dollars a year recycling through the U.S. economy rather than through the economies of Iran, Russia, and Venezuela."

Friends

The executive is ready to leave for lunch when his secretary buzzes him.

"A man who says he's your investment banker is here with two friends. He wants to know if you'd like to join them for lunch," she announced.

"That's impossible. He has to be lying about who he is," the executive answers.

"Why do you say that?"

"Whoever heard of an investment banker with friends?"

Short takes

Whenever new employees come on board at her company, the CEO makes a point to spend a few minutes with them. Her chat with them usually ends with asking them to make a conscious decision what kind of employee they will be: (1) one who makes things happen, (2) one who watches things happen, or (3) one who wonders what happened.

A Jesuit priest wanted a cigarette while he prayed, and decided to ask their bishop for permission to smoke as he prayed. The priest was firmly told no.

A little while later he spotted a fellow priest who was happily smoking, and asked him, "Why did the Bishop allow you to smoke and not me?"

"Because you asked if you could smoke while you prayed and I asked if I could pray while I smoked!" the second priest replied.

Memorable quotes

"Swipe from the best, then adapt." - *Tom Peters*

"Sit, walk, or run, but don't wobble." - *Zen proverb*

"I will act as if what I do will make a difference."
- *William James*

"Remember, a dead fish can float down a stream,
but it takes a live one to swim upstream."
- *W.C. Fields*

"If the only tool you have is a hammer, you tend to
see every problem as a nail." - *Abraham Maslow*

"Not everything that counts can be counted, and
not everything that can be counted counts."
- *Albert Einstein*

"Discovery is seeing what everybody else has seen,
and thinking what nobody else has thought."
- *Albert Szent-Gyorgi*

"A pile of rocks ceases to be a rock pile when
somebody contemplates it with the idea of a ca-
thedral in mind." - *Antoine Saint-Exupery*

"Without a deadline, baby, I wouldn't do nothing." - *Duke Ellington*

The worst excuses overheard from someone caught napping

They told me at the blood drive that this might happen.

This business book I've been reading suggested I take a power nap at this time each day.

I was just doing what you told me: working smarter – not harder.

I wasn't sleeping; I was meditating on the mission statement and envisioning a new paradigm.

I haven't read the book yet, but I heard this is one of the habits of highly effective people.

This is comp time for the three hours last night that I thought about work.

It's not my fault that the coffee machine is broken.

The mailman "went postal" so I was playing dead to avoid getting shot.

Thoughts to manage by

"Statistics suggest that when customers complain, business owners and managers ought to get excited about it. The complaining customer represents a huge opportunity for more business."
- *Zig Ziglar*

"The people here at Google are young. Every day there are lots of new challenges. I keep things focused. The speech I give every day is: 'This is what we do. Is what you are doing consistent with that, and does it change the world?'"
- *Eric Schmidt*

"You can't expect your employees to exceed the expectations of your customers if you don't exceed the employees' expectations of management."
- *Howard Schultz*

"Hiring people is an art, not a science, and resumes can't tell you whether someone will fit into a company's culture. When you realize you've made a mistake, you need to cut your losses and move on." - *Howard Schultz*

"I have yet to find the man, however exalted his station, who did not do better work and put forth greater effort under a spirit of approval than under a spirit of criticism." - *Charles Schwab*

"Well, yes, I've fired a lot of people. Generally I like other people to do it, because it's always a lousy task. But I have fired many people."
- *Donald Trump*

"My main job was developing talent. I was a gardener providing water and other nourishment to our top 750 people. Of course, I had to pull out some weeds, too." - *Jack Welch*

"People ask me, how is managing in the New Economy different from managing in the Old Economy? Actually, it's a lot the same. It's about the financial discipline of the bottom line, understanding your customers, segmenting your customers by their needs, and building a world-class management team." - *Meg Whitman*

"Good management consists in showing average people how to do the work of superior people."
- *John D. Rockefeller*

Things we can learn from our dogs

When a loved one comes home, always go to the door to greet them.

Let others know when they've invaded your territory.

Spend some time each day running and playing.

Always demonstrate loyalty to those who are important to you.

If you want something important that is buried, keep digging until you find it.

When someone close to you had a bad day, show them some concern and affection.

Avoid biting when just a growl will do.

When you're happy, don't be afraid to let the whole world know it.

No matter how often you're scolded, don't pout for too long.

Delight in the simple joys of a walk around the block.

Innovation

"If you are content with the best you have done, you will never do the best you can do."
- *Martin Vanbee*

"The way to get good ideas is to get lots of ideas and throw the bad ones away."
- *Linus Pauling*

"Ideas won't keep. Something must be done about them." - *Alfred North Whitehead*

Fortune 500 trivia

Since 1955, only three companies have held the number one spot on the Fortune 500. They are General Motors (37 years, last time in 2001), Exxon (13 times) and Wal-Mart (9 times).

Mark Zuckerberg of facebook is currently the youngest Fortune 500 CEO (born in 1984). He is nine years younger than the second youngest CEO, Marissa Mayer of Yahoo.

Priceline.com is the newest member of the Fortune 500, joining the list in 2013.

If the Fortune 500 were a country, their combined sales of $12.2 trillion would make them the second largest economy in the world, behind the U.S. but ahead of China, whose economy totals $8.2 trillion in sales.

The largest annual loss of all time for a Fortune 500 company was AIG; the corporation lost $99 billion in 2008.

There are 57 companies in the Fortune 500 who made the initial list in 1955 and have been on the Fortune 500 every year since then.

Thoughts about success

"I'm a success today because I had a friend who believed in me and I didn't have the heart to let him down." — *Abraham Lincoln*

"Have no fear of perfection - you'll never reach it." — *Salvador Dalí*

"Don't spend time beating on a wall, hoping to transform it into a door."
— *Coco Chanel*

"Our greatest glory is not that we never fall, but in rising every time we fall."
— *Confucius*

More amazingly wrong predictions

"Before man reaches the moon, mail will be delivered within hours from New York to Australia by guided missiles. We stand on the threshold of rocket mail."
Arthur Summerfield, U.S. Postmaster General, in 1959

"Atomic energy might be as good as our present-day explosives, but it is unlikely to produce anything very much more dangerous."
Winston Churchill in 1939

Robert Metcalfe is the founder of the 3Com company, a professor at The University of Texas, holds a PhD from Harvard, and is the co-inventor of the Ethernet. Despite his impressive resume, Robert Metcalfe is known for at least one terribly inaccurate prediction. In a 1995 issue of *InfoWorld*, he predicted that the internet "will soon go spectacularly supernova and in 1996 catastrophically collapse." Two years later, during his keynote speech at the WWW International Conference, he held up a magazine page containing the quote to the audience, put it in a blender, and literally ate his words.

"Whatever happens, the U.S. Navy is not going to be caught napping."
Frank Knox, U.S. Secretary of the Navy, on December 4, 1941, three days before the attack on Pearl Harbor

Business ideas to use

How to give a captivating speech

Whether talking to a classroom of third graders or a roomful of executives as keynote speaker, the same principles apply. Below are some guidelines to giving a speech that's memorable for all the right reasons:

The first step should always be to *define the goal of your speech*. What do you want the audience to get out of it?

When writing the speech, *put yourself in the position of the audience*. Why do they care about the topic? What is it about the topic that will pique their interest?

Keep it simple. Trying to cover too many points may result in an audience forgetting the whole content.

There is no need to write out the speech word for word – it encourages reading the speech. Using an *outline or bullet points* will make the speech sound more spontaneous and natural.

A*void memorizing the speech*. First, it's more diffi-cult and time consuming to prepare that way. Sec-ond, it sounds less natural to the audience. Third, memorizing raises pre-speech jitters due to worrying about not only the content, but if you will flub it by forgetting your lines.

Practice your speech several times, out loud if possible.

Try to *visit the venue ahead of time*. It will make you feel more comfortable when the time comes.

Avoid the temptation to put the spotlight on slides or other distractions. *The speaker should be the focal point.*

Do not use acronyms or buzzwords, unless you are certain that every last person in the audience will understand them.

Creativity and innovation

"Intuition will tell the thinking mind where to look next." - *Jonas Salk*

"If you have always done it that way, it is probably wrong." - *Charles Kettering*

"We don't see things as they are, we see things as *we* are." - *Anais Nin*

"There is only one thing stronger than all the armies of the world: and that is an idea whose time has come." - *Victor Hugo*

"If you lose the power to laugh, you lose the power to think." - *Clarence Darrow*

"Ideas are like rabbits. You get a couple and learn how to handle them, and pretty soon you have a dozen." - *John Steinbeck*

"It is the essence of genius to make use of the simplest ideas." - *Charles Peguy*

"If you can dream it, you can do it." - *Walt Disney*

How to say "no" like a pro

Every time management guru and self-help book touts the importance of refusing requests that are drains on time and energy. The problem is that saying "no" can be difficult and awkward, which is why many people follow the path of least resistance and say "yes," only to regret it afterwards.

E. B. White (short for Elwyn Brooks) was an American writer best known for the popular children's book *Charlotte's Web*. He also co-authored the English language style guide, *The Elements of Style*, which is commonly known as *Strunk & White*.

E.B. White was also a master at saying "no." The letter below, written in 1956, was an example where he said no graciously and used a splash of humor to temper his refusal. He wrote:

Dear Mr. Adams,

How wonderful to hear from you! Thanks for your invitation to join the committee of the Arts and Sciences for Eisenhower.

I must decline, for secret reasons.

Sincerely,

E.B. White

White's response demonstrates a simple formula that can be used to respond to every request you want to refuse:

Step 1: Affirm the value of the relationship to you, by saying something like, "It really is good to hear from you."

Step 2: Thank the person sincerely for the opportunity with a statement like, "I am honored that you thought of me."

Step 3: Decline firmly and politely, for instance, "However, at this time several factors make it necessary for me to decline."

Quotes on leadership

"Leaders must be close enough to relate to others, but far enough ahead to motivate them." - *John C. Maxwell*

"You can change only what people know, not what they do." - *Scott Adams, Author of God's Debris: A Thought Experiment*

"The show doesn't go on because it's ready; it goes on because it's 11:30." - *Lorne Michaels about Saturday Night Live*

"No great manager or leader ever fell from heaven; it's learned, not inherited."
- *Tom Northup*

"Make your top managers rich and they will make you rich." - *Robert H. Johnson*

"The best executive is the one who has sense enough to pick good men to do what he wants done, and self-restraint to keep from meddling with them while they do it."
- *Theodore Roosevelt*

***Watch for these other Bathroom Companion
books coming soon...***

Investor's Bathroom Companion

Teacher's Bathroom Companion

Banker's Bathroom Companion

Nurse's Bathroom Companion

Physician's Bathroom Companion

Golfer's Bathroom Companion

Football Fan's Bathroom Companion

Baseball Fan's Bathroom Companion

Mother's Bathroom Companion

Salesperson's Bathroom Companion

Father's Bathroom Companion

Free Bonus Book Excerpt

Slaying Season
A Jake Goodman Action Mystery

By James Laabs

Available in soft cover or Kindle at Amazon.com

Chapter One

The Athletic Director looked at the resume for the fifti-eth time and, try as he might, could find nothing to dis-like about Jacob "Jake" Goodman. He had the brains, a commendable service record in the Marines, good looks and came from a solid family. If only there was a giant red flag that popped out – then he'd have a reason to not hire the kid. That would make life a lot easier, since he would have loved to use the Sports Information Director job opening to pay back one of the many favors that needed paying back.

As it was, Jake Goodman was the only son of one of the top financial backers of Lincoln State University. And when it came to doing favors for large donors to univer-sity athletics, money didn't just talk – it shouted.

Turning back to Jake Goodman's resume, he ticked off the points. Goodman had a degree in journalism from good old Lincoln State, so he was an alumnus. Not a necessity but a strong point in his favor. Jake was white, and although the Athletic Director would deny it with his last breath, there was no way he was hiring anyone of color into a responsible position in the athletic department. In the little corner of the university that Harvey Elwood ruled, the color of authority was lily white and that's how Harvey planned to keep it.

Harvey sighed loudly as he pictured what would happen if he backed another candidate. Jake's father would go crying straight to the Board of Trustees and Harvey would make a fool out himself trying to defend any other choice. Jake Goodman had an immaculate background and was qualified enough that his father's clout pushed him to the top of the heap for the Sports Information Director position.

The Athletic Director had even gone so far as to hire (with cash so there wouldn't be a trail) a private eye who he sometimes used for discrete dirt-digging. The P.I. came up empty. In fact, the investigative report was so boring that it almost put him to sleep. This kid was a straight arrow – not so much as a speeding ticket. Since Jake had returned from his tour of duty in Iraq three months earlier, he behaved like a priest. He drank an occasional beer now and then, but when he found himself at a party where weed and coke came out he politely declined and found a reason to leave early.

There was no question. When it came down to it, no other candidate matched up nearly as well as Jake Goodman. Harvey was stuck, and he would be unable to pay back any favors with this hire.

Harvey was about to let out another sigh when there was a knock on his door. "Come in!" he shouted. It was

Molly Bennett, the person who managed the women's athletic department. The athletic department was split in two, with two Assistant Directors. One was responsible for men's sports and one for women's sports, and both reported to Harvey. Although he and Molly didn't see eye-to-eye on a lot of things, he respected her because she was a very competent administrator, a quality that was sorely needed on the women's sports side of the department. It took a hard-nose like Molly to stretch miniscule budgets and build support for sports that didn't draw flies when it came to paid attendance.

"So, how is it going with the Sports Information Director position?" Molly asked, "Have you made a decision?"

Harvey slid Jake's resume across his spacious mahogany desk toward her. "Here's our man – Jake Goodman. He's the offspring of Stan Goodman, one of Lincoln State's biggest contributors."

Molly scanned the resume quickly while she mumbled. "Hmmm...degree from Lincoln State, good...war hero, huh? That'll sit well with our older alum...I see he did a couple of internships with the *Peoria Journal-Star* and the WICS-TV sports department here in Springfield. That will help. Not as much experience as I'd like to see, but he looks like a decent choice, Harvey. Let's get him on the payroll so we can start getting some stuff in the paper about women's soccer. The season starts in a few weeks and it's one of my only sports that actually sells a few tickets."

"I'm bringing him in to talk about a job offer tomorrow. But I wanted to make sure you're on board with this."

"He looks great to me, what did Milt have to say about him?" Molly asked. Milt Atkins was – at least in title –

her equal, responsible for overseeing the day-to-day operations of the men's side of the department. In reality, Harvey kept Milt under his thumb and made the decisions, relegating Milt to being a well-paid paper pusher.

"Milt isn't a part of this decision, Molly, so if he doesn't like it he can go screw himself."

Molly gave a tiny evil smile. It was time to tease old Harvey a little, which she enjoyed doing, "Or he may go running to the Board of Trustees to squeal on you, he certainly isn't afraid to do that."

Harvey frowned, "The next time he goes over my head, it will be his last official act as an Assistant Director. I'll demote him so far down he'll be reporting to the little girls who peddle popcorn at your soccer games."

Molly laughed, "You know what, Harvey? I believe you'd do it. Milt has been a thorn in your side from the first day you met him. And you wouldn't have an argument from me. In fact, I could use the change of scenery and handle men's sports instead of pinching pennies with the girls."

"And you would be damn good at it too, Molly. I'll keep you in mind if and when I can shake Milt loose from the department. In the meantime, go count some soccer balls or something and let me get back to work."

Molly took Harvey's good natured dismissal with a smile. "OK, Harv. Bring the kid over to meet me when he's ready to get to work."

"The annual kickoff picnic is next Saturday," Harvey said, "I figured that would be a good place to have him meet everyone."

The kickoff picnic was usually held on the Saturday before registration began for the fall semester, before the non-athlete student body descended on the campus. It was a chance for athletes in all sports to cut loose a bit and get themselves in a frame of mind to attend class, study and play at top level in their chosen sport (although not necessarily in that order).

Harvey picked up the phone and dialed Jake Goodman's cell phone. "Jake! Harvey Elwood here. I'd like you to come over tomorrow morning. I want to make you the new Sports Information Director for Lincoln State."

Jake put down the phone, smiled with satisfaction and gave a subdued fist pump. The Lincoln State job was a perfect place to start his career. The only reservation he had about taking the job was that his dad had thrown his influence into the hiring process. Jake worried that he would be viewed as some trust-fund punk who relied on his family's wealth and clout to get ahead. People who knew him at all recognized that Jake was determined to make his own way in the world – if the people at Lincoln State thought he was a rich kid slacker who was going to coast on his dad's wealth, they were badly mistaken. That's why he had joined the Marines right after graduation. He wanted to get out from under his dad's massive shadow and the best way to do that was to put his career off for a few years and join the service.

The day he enlisted was still clear in Jake's mind. He had graduated from Lincoln State just the month before and found that job prospects were pretty slim for new grads. Although Jake got top grades, journalism majors outnumbered job openings by about 5-to-1 and a degree from a small school in Springfield, Illinois held zero prestige with the big media outlets in Chicago or St. Louis. After he struck out in the job market, the last thing Jake wanted was to sit around Springfield doing nothing, and since his dad forbade him to take any job that was "beneath him," joining the Marines seemed like the easy way out.

He remembered that it was a sunny, warm summer day when he walked in the door of the family's spacious house and announced he was leaving for boot camp within the week. His mother made a strange gurgling sound, turned ashen white and fainted; Jake still shuddered when he recalled the clunk her head made when she hit the floor. His father paused from screaming at him for a few seconds when she fell, took a quick glance to make sure his wife was conscious (she was) and then resumed his tirade. Of course, Stan Goodman offered to "pull some strings" and persuade someone to misplace Jake's enlistment papers. Jake's refusal of that offer was received with bulging neck veins and even louder shouting by his father.

It turned out that the Marines was as positive an experience as fighting in a war could be. Jake returned home with a small box full of medals and felt like he had taken a huge step toward proving his own worth, independent of his family. He also had the good fortune of picking up some excellent experience working for the Marine's public information office for five months. Jake injured his leg in battle and a commanding officer, who had taken a liking to him, assigned him to journalism duty until he was ready to return to his unit. Taglines on quite a few stories read "by Jake Goodman," and those would hopefully prove invaluable in landing a journalism job. Jake was brimming with confidence and optimism when he was discharged.

Now he landed the Sports Information Director position for a Division I athletic program; a job that anyone would grab in a second as the starting point for a journalism career. Obviously his father had put in a good word for him, but Jake could live with that.

Jake pulled into a parking spot marked "reserved for athletic department staff only," slammed the door of his hybrid sports car, checked his tie in the side mirror, and walked into the athletic offices. The colors of the Abes (the Lincoln State nickname, for Abraham Lincoln who was born in the area) were royal blue and gray, so the reception area was covered in rich blue carpet with gray highlights. To his left, Jake noticed a floor-to-ceiling glass case with several sports trophies won by the Abes over the years.

"Jake Goodman, to see Harvey Elwood," his said, flashing his brightest smile at the receptionist. It's never too early to start winning people over, he thought. The cute, thirty-ish receptionist gave her best smile back and said, "Go right in Jake, he's expecting you."

Harvey Elwood's office was spacious and recently redecorated. As Jake shook hands with Harvey and sat down, he couldn't help but be impressed with the view from the huge window. The athletic department offices were in a building located just off one of the corners of the football stadium. The building was built with a small footprint but was four stories tall. Harvey's corner office on the top floor overlooked the stadium and football field. Of course, blue and gray dominated the décor'; Jake played a mental game to count the items in the office that weren't blue or gray and was able to tally them on one hand with fingers to spare. Harvey himself wore a gray suit with a royal blue tie. It brought to mind the joke that Jake's dad told him about Harvey being so loyal to Lincoln State that if he cut himself he'd bleed royal blue instead of red.

The meeting went smoothly. The money was all right and Jake was excited for the chance to go to work for his alma mater. His first introduction to the world of Lincoln State athletic administration would be at the annual kick-off picnic the next day.

Chapter Two

"Are you sorry you got yourself into this yet?" boomed the voice of Donald "Slim" Haskins, head coach of the Lincoln State Abes football team. Jake smiled and paused before answering. Whoever hung the nickname "Slim" on Donald Haskins must have been either blind or had a cruel sense of humor, Jake thought. Haskins was about six feet tall but had 300 pounds packed onto his wide frame.

"Actually I'm looking forward to getting to work," Jake answered politely, "and one of the first things on my list is to work on getting some press for your team. The season starts three weeks from today if I'm not mistaken."

"You got that right, boy. And we need some publicity – season ticket sales dropped off a bit this year so it's up to you to get some asses in those seats."

"That's what I'm here to do, so I'll plan on getting together in your office with you Monday afternoon right after practice ends," Jake said decisively in hopes of ending the conversation as quickly as possible.

"Okeydokey. See you then, junior."

Just then, a familiar face ambled up to him and Haskins. Jake recognized him as Steve Jefferies, the men's basketball coach for the Abes. Steve Jefferies was polar opposite of Slim Haskins. He was tall, good looking and in great shape. He also had a personality that was both easy going but serious at the same time. He was well-spoken and intelligent with just the right touch of genuine enthusiasm about the university and his basketball team.

The results of the two teams also were exact opposites: The football team was coming off a 1-and-10 season while the Abes basketball team made the "Big Dance" three years running and routinely sold out every game while the football team struggled to build a following.

The coaches were both stereotypes in their own way. Slim Haskins was an "old school" coach, one of the last of a dying breed. He was abrasive, didn't get along well with the media, and wasn't particularly liked by alumni, fans or his own players. Haskins was typical of coaches that were fast being replaced by a new generation of coaches like Steve Jefferies.

The new breed of coaches studied psychology and public relations to better handle their players, the media, fans and the wide range of other people they came in contact with as a major college coach. Slim Haskins was a dinosaur and everyone, from the Board of Trustees to Slim himself, knew it. This was the last year of his contract, and Slim Haskins realized that it would take a great year to keep his job after this season.

Jake couldn't help but notice that the tension between Haskins and Steve Jefferies was extremely high.

"So Steve-O," Slim said, "I saw your star forward driving a new SUV last week. I wonder how he got himself such a nice car."

"He saved the money from his summer job for a down payment," Steve Jefferies answered calmly, "the first thing I did when I saw him with it was ask him how he got it. Then I made some calls to verify his story and it checked out. That's how we do things – on my team players know they're accountable. You ought to try it sometime."

Haskins' round face flushed bright red, "Well, yeah, it's easy for you to keep tabs on fifteen players; I have over ninety players on the football team that I have to keep in line."

"You also have eight assistant coaches to help you."

Jake didn't want to be caught in the middle of a discussion that was growing more heated by the moment, so he interrupted. "Coach Jefferies, I've already set up a meeting to go over the publicity plan for football this year," he said, "as soon as I get the fall sports going and the dust settles we should get together about basketball."

"That works for me," Steve Jefferies said, just as eager to avoid a shouting match with Slim Haskins in front of the entire athletic department, "give me a call in a few weeks."

Slim Haskins used the opportunity to stomp off in the direction of the beer keg, and Steve Jefferies ambled off in another direction. Molly Bennett took the opportunity to introduce herself to Jake.

"Just the man I need to get to know," Molly said with a smile as she thrust out her hand. "I'm Molly Bennett, women's assistant A.D. We have a lot of work to do in a very short amount of time."

"I couldn't agree more," Jake said. As they chatted, Jake recalled his father's assessment of the key people in the athletic department. Dad seemed to have missed the mark on Molly Bennett, who he described to Jake as "a humorless broad with a giant chip on her shoulder." On the contrary, Jake's first impression was that Molly was funny, competent and very smart. They agreed to meet first thing Monday morning in her office.

As he talked with Molly, Jake noticed Harvey Elwood walking away from the picnic area, heading down the trail that led to the crew team's boathouse. The Lincoln State campus was adjacent to a small lake which the crew teams used for rowing practice, and the boathouse was nestled in the trees by the shore. The University was surprisingly a national power in the sport of crew, thanks to a world-class facility funded by a graduate who rowed for Lincoln State while in college and hit it big in the 1990s in computer software.

A slight, skinny man in his late forties approached Jake and Molly. He was wearing gray shorts with a royal blue Lincoln State t-shirt and had a broad smile on his face. "Jake, I'm Milt Atkins, the Assistant Athletic Director. Glad to have you with us."

"One of two Assistant Athletic Directors," Molly said, "the other one would be me."

Milt Atkins laughed good-naturedly, "How could I ever forget, Molly? You remind me several times a week. Jake, we are looking forward to seeing what you can do, especially for the football program. Hopefully you'll do better than your predecessor."

Molly and Jake both grimaced. Everyone in the athletic department knew the story of the previous Sports Information Director at Lincoln State and how his career ended.

Football attendance the previous year was dismal, with the stands half-full for many games. Students, normally the most loyal attendees, were not even showing up. They had discovered it was more fun to drink at their frat house or local bar than to sneak booze into the stadium and be subjected to another woeful performance by the Abes.

With pressure mounting to boost attendance, the desperate Sports Information Director came up with a creative idea to promote the next home game: he convinced the Springfield Zoo to co-sponsor a "Day at the Zoo" event at the football game. How could it go wrong? The zoo would get some publicity and dads could drag their kids to the game and kill two birds with one stone; watch a football game and let the kids see some zoo animals.

As the players left the field at halftime, the zookeepers paraded their animals onto the artificial turf. It was a grand and amazing sight as an elephant, tiger, zebra, horses and a dozen other animals pranced around the playing field. Unfortunately, no one anticipated the obvious result of having several nervous large animals in a confined area. As the beasts were led off the playing surface, they left behind enormous piles of poop. Giant turd mounds littered the field like smelly land mines.

Since getting the zoo animals on and off the field had used up all of the time allotted for the halftime break, the referees and media producers were calling for the game to start the moment the last animal stepped out of the stadium. In the meantime, athletic department interns were dispatched to find buckets, water, hoses, anything that could possibly be used to clean the field. Their frantic efforts resulted in perhaps one-tenth of the meadow muffins being removed, but many piles remained as the teams lined up for the second half kick-off.

Very few people remember the score, or even who won the game. But the second half would go down in history as one of the low points of the athletic program at Lincoln State University. Players were streaked with zoo animal *ordure* and fans in the lower rows of seats gagged on the smell. Coaches were holding towels doused with analgesic rub over their faces to try to mask the horrendous odor. The newspaper reported sightings of small children in the stands vomiting the soda and popcorn they had consumed during the first half. The most memorable play involved a player from the opposing team stretching to catch a pass, making the catch and then sliding on his belly for fifteen yards through a wet turd pile, leaving a long, brown streak on the field.

The Sports Information Director was excused from his position the very next day by unanimous vote at a special Sunday morning meeting of the Athletic Board. Harvey was chastised by the Board but shifted the vast majority of the blame with some smooth talking and finger pointing. He was so shell-shocked that he assigned Sports Information duties to various administrators and put off hiring a new S.I.D. and promotions manager until the following summer.

***

Harvey took a quick look over his shoulder as he approached the boathouse. No one had followed him down the trail from the picnic area. He pulled his keys from his pocket, quickly unlocked the door and stepped inside. Suddenly two arms and two legs wrapped around him from behind and he felt a wet, warm tongue in his ear. "Did'ja miss me?" asked Jennifer Stewart.

"Can't you tell?" he replied as he removed her from his back, spun her around and thrust his hips into her.

"Oooh, yes…I can tell!"

Harvey gently pushed Jennifer into the pile of nylon boat covers that were in the corner of the large room. Sleek wooden boats that were little more than empty hulls and a hundred oars of various lengths were stored all around the room on steel racks. The outside walls had a few windows but Harvey and Jennifer felt secure knowing that no one had any reason to be anywhere near the boathouse on this day.

This was the first time they had seen one another in over two months and there was little foreplay. Jennifer moaned with pleasure as Harvey entered her and within a few minutes both of them had climaxed explosively. Now they lay in the pile of nylon fabric, entwined and both still breathing hard.

"Welcome back to the new school year, and congratulations on your promotion to Graduate Assistant to the Athletic Director," Harvey said.

Harvey had met Jennifer two years before, when she was a junior captain of the women's volleyball team. He was immediately struck by her unique good looks and maturity. Jennifer was everything that a fifty-year-old man needed. She was personable, fun, mature for her age and a sexual dynamo, at least compared to Harvey's near-frigid wife. Best of all, Jennifer understood discretion – a key attribute in a mistress if one was a married, high profile public figure.

When they started their affair, Jennifer accepted immediately that this was a fling with no long-term chance of leading somewhere. She was in her second year of grad school and would almost certainly leave in spring to start a career hundreds of miles away. She lived in the moment with no expectations about the future of their relationship, and that was one of the things that made her so attractive to Harvey.

As they lay on the soft nylon, sexually spent and totally relaxed, both heard a sound that came from one of the windows. Harvey quickly got up, pulled on his underwear and hurried to the window. There was nothing and no one outside that Harvey could see. "Probably just a pine cone or a branch hit the window," he said to Jennifer. Yet, throughout the rest of the day he couldn't get rid of the feeling that someone had been watching them.

Slaying Season
By James Laabs

Available at Amazon.com in soft cover or Kindle

Printed in Great Britain
by Amazon.co.uk, Ltd.,
Marston Gate.